D0504945

GEORGE MOORE
LETTERS TO LADY CUNARD

Maud Alice Burke, 1894

[*Frontispiece*

GEORGE MOORE

Letters to Lady Cunard
1895–1933

Edited
with an introduction and notes
by Rupert Hart-Davis

Rupert Hart-Davis
Soho Square London
1957

PRINTED AND BOUND IN ENGLAND BY
HAZELL WATSON AND VINEY LTD
AYLESBURY AND LONDON

ILLUSTRATIONS

INTRODUCTION

(1)

GEORGE MOORE took a great interest in the writing of his life and was at pains to instruct his biographer elect. When John Eglinton held that position, Moore made more than one journey to Bournemouth to put Eglinton "right on two points in his life which he considered important. One of these was the definite ambition, avowed to Zola, with which he had returned from Paris to England, of winning 'freedom' for English fiction. The other was the story of a grand passion."[1]

When Eglinton withdrew and Charles Morgan was chosen in his place, Moore told Morgan that "the most valuable existing source, outside his own memory and his autobiographical writings, was a certain series of letters addressed by him to a single correspondent".[2] This, Morgan discovered, was Lady Cunard. Moore duly introduced them, but when Morgan asked whether he might see the letters, Lady Cunard refused to show them, even as Madame Viardot had refused to show Turgenev's.

After Moore's death Morgan renewed his request, reinforced by a strong wish expressed in Moore's will: it was again refused, and Morgan abandoned the biography, on which he had already spent much time, because without these letters he knew he could not write the book that he and George Moore had planned. The biography was

[1] John Eglinton: *Irish Literary Portraits* (1935), pp. 98–99.
[2] Charles Morgan: *Epitaph on George Moore* (1935), p. 3.

7

eventually written, most ably, by Joseph Hone, but without benefit of the letters to Lady Cunard, except for two which came from other sources. It is impossible to say how many letters there originally were; probably several thousand, for the friendship lasted almost forty years, and Moore was an assiduous correspondent. Moreover, he always refused to have a telephone installed (though in an emergency a telephone message could be relayed to Ebury Street through "the apothecary Hucklebridge" who lived opposite). Presumably Lady Cunard destroyed the rest of the letters, leaving very few from the earlier years. More than half of the 276 letters she bequeathed to Mr Sacheverell Sitwell date from the last decade of Moore's life. He kept few papers, and no letters from Lady Cunard to him have survived.

(2)

In 1894, when almost certainly they first met, George Moore was forty-two. He had been born at Moore Hall in County Mayo and ill-educated, partly in Irish racing stables and partly at the Catholic college of Oscott, near Birmingham. When he was eighteen his father died, and finding himself with an adequate income he went to Paris to become a painter. He lived there for ten years, but failed in his object, though he gained the friendship of Manet, Degas, Zola, Huysmans, Mallarmé, and many other artists and writers. Since 1880 he had lived in London and published two volumes of verse, a play, a savage attack on Ireland called *Parnell and his Island* (1887), a book of essays and one of art criticism, *Confessions of a Young Man* (1888) the first of his autobiographical studies, and seven novels. His eighth, *Esther Waters* (March 1894), which won for English fiction a great deal of the freedom its author desired, and has been consistently read ever since, was a new book at the time of his meeting with the future Lady Cunard. Always a great lover of women, though how satisfactorily will never be known, he had recently been paying unsuccessful court to Mrs Pearl Craigie, who wrote as John Oliver Hobbes and with whom he had collaborated in the writing of plays.[1]

(3)

Maud Alice Burke was born of wealthy parents in San Francisco on 31 August 1872. It is impossible to verify this, since all records were destroyed in the earthquake of 1906, but it was the date she gave at the time of her wedding in 1895, when she seemingly had little reason to falsify her age. Later in life she usually subtracted five years.

Little is known of her youth, except that she spent a considerable part of it in Europe, presumably with her mother. Her father died when she was in her teens, and her mother remarried. In 1893 Maud was engaged to Prince André Poniatowski of Poland, with whom she was passionately in love, but he is believed to have jilted her, and on the rebound she married Sir Bache Cunard, with whom she had nothing whatever in common.

They were married in New York on 17 April 1895 and three days later sailed for England. Sir Bache was forty-three, a member of the shipping family, and the second

[1] *The Fool's Hour*, the first act of a comedy by John Oliver Hobbes and George Moore, appeared in the first issue of the *Yellow Book* (April 1894). *Journeys End in Lovers Meeting*, a proverb in one act by the same authors, was produced by Ellen Terry as a curtain-raiser at Daly's Theatre on 5 June 1894 with herself, Johnston Forbes-Robertson and William Terriss in the cast, and kept in her repertory for several years. Although G.M. appeared as co-author on the programme, the play was eventually published in John Oliver Hobbes's *Tales about Temperaments* (1902) without mention of his name.

9

Baronet. He was fond of hunting and owned a large house called Nevill Holt, near Market Harborough in Leicestershire. Here the young Lady Cunard was installed, and her daughter Nancy was born in 1896. Lady Cunard soon discovered her gifts as a hostess, and the Nevill Holt visitors book for the next fifteen years was filled with the names of the rich and famous. In 1911 Lady Cunard parted from Sir Bache, left Nevill Holt for ever, and lived for the rest of her life in London. Sir Bache died in 1925, but his widow never remarried.

(4)

How did George Moore fit into this picture? When and where did he and Maud Burke first meet? Before her marriage, almost certainly in 1894, perhaps in May, and probably at the Savoy Hotel. Moore himself said so, in the 1921 edition of *Memoirs of my Dead Life*, though that in itself cannot be taken as proof:

> I . . . stood there unconscious that my cure [for his unhappy love affair with Pearl Craigie] was coming towards me and that I should find it on the terrace outside overlooking the river in the Savoy Hotel, whither I must go at once, having forgotten to order dinner for the friends who were dining with me the next day.

John Eglinton was given some additional details, which do not necessarily conflict with that account:

> One day, when he was lunching in some fashionable restaurant, a lively party entered, and Moore, who was known to some of its members, was haled over to their table, where he exerted himself to entertain the company. Seated opposite to him was a brilliant young lady, destined to become one of the principal figures in society, who listened delightedly to his sallies, and with a sudden inspiration called out to him, "George Moore, you have a soul of fire!" It was the compliment of his life, the re-

membrance of which he constantly cherished, and the incident was the beginning of a romantic attachment, all that was wanted to complete the sentimental equipment of this Balzacian young Irishman.[1]

Nancy Cunard remembers that when Moore told her the story, he described how Maud arranged to sit next to him.[2]

What is certain is that Maud Burke was wearing a pink-and-grey shot-silk dress, and that George Moore fell in love with her at first sight.

(5)

Few writers have so tightly interwoven fact and fiction as George Moore did in his autobiographical works. Naturally inaccurate in detail, he would transpose dates, events and people in any way that suited his artistic purpose, though the more one studies the books in conjunction with the known incidents of Moore's life, the more certainly do even the most outrageous anecdotes appear to rest on a substratum of fact. Nevertheless, the quotations that follow must be read as indications rather than positive evidence.

The book that concerns us most is *Memoirs of my Dead Life*, the first autobiographical book that Moore wrote after 1894. Each time a new edition gave him the opportunity, he rewrote parts of the book extensively, adding or removing whole sections, so that it is necessary to consult every edition from 1906 to 1928 to find all the references to his love for Lady Cunard. In the first edition (1906) she figures only obliquely in the final section called *Resurgam*, in which Moore tells how he was summoned to his mother's deathbed at Moore Hall.

---

[1] Eglinton, p. 100.
[2] G.M.: *Memories of George Moore* (1956), p. 114.

While he was waiting for the hearse and carriages to arrive he walked out to the shore of Lough Carra and meditated:

> A man cannot lament two women at the same time, and only a month ago the most beautiful thing that had ever appeared in my life, an idea which I knew from the first I was destined to follow, had appeared to me, had stayed with me for a while, and had passed from me. All the partial loves of my youth seemed to find expression at last in a passion that would know no change. Who shall explain the mystery of love that time cannot change? Fate is the only word that conveys any idea of it, for of what use to say that her hair was blonde and thick, that her eyes were grey and blue? I had known many women before her, and many had hair and eyes as fine and as deep as hers, but never one but she had had the indispensable quality of making me feel I was more intensely alive when she was by me than I was when she was away.

This passage, which was substantially retained in every edition, can be accepted as exactly true, even to the phrase "only a month ago," since Mrs Moore died on 25 May 1895, and Maud Burke had been married on 17 April.

Later that same year (1906) appeared the Tauchnitz edition of the *Memoirs*, in which the first section of the book (originally called *Spring in London*) is greatly enlarged and retitled *Theme and Variations*. Here Maud appears as Elizabeth: "I can think of nothing more like her than a bird, for she has the bright eyes of a bird, and she is instinctive and courageous as a sparrow-hawk."

But before pursuing her further in this edition, there is another document that must be consulted. It consists of some manuscript pages which, Moore said, were stolen and sold by one of his secretaries. They appeared in a bookseller's catalogue in 1913, were later sold at auction in the United States, and eventually found their way into the hands of a New York dealer, who some time during the 1920s, without Moore's knowledge, had them set up and printed in the same type as the first edition of the *Memoirs* and gave away copies to his customers. Gradually, in America at any rate, these pages have come to be known as the "suppressed chapter" of *Memoirs of my Dead Life*, though careful scrutiny makes it certain that they were in fact an incomplete and rejected draft of the new material which Moore added to the Tauchnitz edition in 1906.[1] The draft is more lush and less restrained than the published version, but it contains some additional incidents, and since the two versions do not conflict in the smallest detail, I here quote from them indiscriminately. First, of their meeting:

> The body envolumes the soul, and a shot-silk shimmered in the May sunlight when she came forward and put her little hand, like a fern and white as a lily, into mine.

Of her character:

> Her courage, independence, her intellectual audacity, no doubt captured my admiration. . . . I admired her cold sensuality, cold because it was divorced from tenderness and passion. . . . I loved but an immortal goddess descended once more among men. Her sensuality was so serene and so sure of its divine character that it never seemed to become trivial or foolish. While walking in the woods with one, she would say: "Let us sit here," and after looking steadily at one for a few seconds, her pale marmoreal eyes glowing, she would say, "You can make love to me now, if you like".

Of the course of their love:

> Again I hear the soft sound of the door opening over the velvet pile of carpet. It does not follow that because a woman sometimes reminds one of a dryad that she does not at other times remind one of Boucher or Fragonard, and that

[1] The manuscript of these pages is now in the collection of Mr Arthur A. Houghton Jr.

night Elizabeth seemed to me a very Fragonard, a plump Fragonard maiden as she sat up in bed reading, her gold hair in plaits and a large book in her hand. I asked her what she was reading, and might have talked literature for a while, but throwing the vain linen aside she revealed herself, and in that moment of august nakedness the mortal woman was forgotten. I saw the eternal spirit shining through her like a lamp hidden in an alabaster vase. That night the mortal woman glowed with immortality.

We may not marry Elizabeth, we may not marry her. Man in his combat with Nature, trying to overcome her laws, invented marriage, and put women into cages thinking to keep them, but they evaporate through the bars as the mist through the reeds. Their bodies remain, but a body without a soul is a wearisome thing. What I am saying is the wisdom of the world, the oldest wisdom, yet few know it. I always knew it, and that is why we did not marry, Elizabeth and I. We knew quite well, from the first, that we were like two ships, lying side by side in the harbour, waiting for the moment when the magnetism of the ocean would draw us forth. That is how Nietzsche words it, speaking of himself and Wagner. Each had a course and a destination to follow, and our eyes saddened one day in the Basque country whither we had gone to verify our impressions of a certain author. . . .
"If we were married we should be very happy—for six months."
"Only for six months?" I answered, admiring her lawlessness. "Is it then decreed that I shall lose you? It is not then your destiny to watch my back broadening as I lean over a desk writing novels. You have come into this life to shine in society, to be a light, to form a salon and to gather clever men round you."
So did I speak to her, and we were sad that beautiful November in the Basque country. But even as I she had a course and a destination, and I knew well it would have been selfish to delay her. Wiser by far it would be to seek a husband for her, a spring-board from which she could leap. And always with this idea in my mind our love story was lived out in Paris. In Heidelberg we spent a delicious morn-

ing on the ramparts overlooking the plain of Germany; we travelled in Holland seeing cathedrals and pictures; and when three months later we returned to England she hired, at my suggestion, one of those wilful little houses [in Park Lane] beloved by me. For a month we sat together nearly every night on that verandahed balcony. It was in one of those nooky little drawing-rooms that our last love scene was enacted.

The question was whom she should marry—who of all the people we knew could supply her with the spring-board she required. I mentioned a name and her eyes brightened. "Do you think so?" Then I knew my hour had sounded. Things of this kind move speedily when they begin to move, and it was in one of those wilful little houses that she said to me, one midnight, "Swear to me that whatever happens, we shall always be friends." I swore it and begged her to tell me what was in her mind. The air seemed ominous, and there was sadness in her and a shroud of evil on the night. What did we do but sink into love of each other's bodies, seeking forgetfulness of the fate about to take us apart.

Then he links Elizabeth with the unnamed girl in *Resurgam*, and tells how he came back from his mother's funeral to meet again "my Elizabeth, now alas! a married woman". Perhaps, he wondered, "if I had only taken her in my arms instead of wasting time speaking to her of literature!" But the opportunity passed, and they next met in a country house party, to which she had apparently arranged his invitation. Once again his hopes were dashed: "she was four months gone, as the saying is," and all his "beseeching" went unrewarded.

"Then why have you come here?" "For torture's sake," and it seemed that she took pleasure in my suffering. Even this is not certain, for she turned her head aside, that she might not see my tears. . . . This woman who had rescued me from one great grief had plunged me into a second. . . . Every night she locked her door when her maid left her, and the sound is and will ever be in my ears.

15

They did not meet again for two years, and then one Sunday afternoon he was driving in a hansom through deserted streets towards Kensington:

> She came towards me in another hansom, young and joyous, tremulous and slight, having regained her figure completely—her baby was then two years old, and her hair seemed thicker and more brilliant, more like real gold than ever, and as I stood talking to her the thought passed that we were not far from my house, and that nothing would be easier than to ask her there to tea. But instead, reader, wilt thou believe me if I tell thee that I asked her to come for a drive . . . where? Wast thou to guess for a thousand years thou couldst not guess my folly. . . . I asked her to come for a drive with me in the Fulham Road! Why the Fulham Road? Because when luck is against us any foolish thing may come into our heads.

> But while I was ascribing my failure to maleficent providence she had begun to steal again into my life, imperceptibly as spring steals into the bleak woodland.

She wrote asking him to stay in the country, and there she said to him: "Well, you've got me again, after all these years." But his was a distant, tenuous hold: the passionate lover gradually turned into the devoted but distant admirer, the faithful correspondent, the hermit of Ebury Street: "my thoughts are now among years of abstinence, years of estrangement." In 1910–11 another took first place in Lady Cunard's affections, but George Moore's devotion was lifelong.

Surprisingly the next major edition of the *Memoirs* (1915) contained none of this new material, and the first section, *Spring in London*, remained exactly as in the original edition. But five years later, in the Author's Edition (New York, 1920) and in the Moore Hall Edition (London, 1921)—these two texts are for our purposes virtually identical—*Spring in London* is enlarged to include an abbreviated and rewritten version of the Tauchnitz *Theme and Variations*. (I have preferred to quote from the earlier versions, since they are fuller and were written nearer the time of the events they describe.) Also a new second section called *Lui et Elles* has been added, in which is described the prelude to his meeting with Elizabeth, his unhappy love for Pearl Craigie (here called Agate), who "prepared the way for the greater love, and served me as Rosaline served Romeo."

These two new sections add little to the story, beyond reaffirming:

> a grey and pink shot silk . . . the day that she came forward in the restaurant, in fine health, high spirits, blonde hair and tiny hands, to insist that I must remain to luncheon with her, and incidentally, with her company:

and finally summing up:

> Elizabeth was a constant but unfaithful mistress; in her own words she "liked not continuity", but was willing to pick up a thread again; and I forgave her certain caprices and take pleasure in remembering that I outlived them all, and that when my poor little reel was empty, when there was no more thread to unwind, a great love passed into a perfect friendship as beautifully and serenely as summer passes into a still autumn, in which all the suffering that she caused me (and she caused me a good deal, for she was terribly egotistical at times) is forgotten, and I remember only the divine recompenses.

The final revisions for the Uniform Edition of 1928 left *Spring in London* substantially unchanged, but *Lui et Elles* was omitted. The whole story hangs together coherently, though in *Vale* (1914), chap. xii, where some scraps of the story are retold, the first meeting, shot-silk dress and all, is placed at Auteuil. No doubt they did meet there, during those first halcyon months, but the weight of evidence places their first meeting in the Savoy Hotel, and the most circumstantial account of the story must be sought in the *Memoirs*, until we reach the pages from *Héloïse and Abélard* which are printed at the end of this book.

(6)

Of the 276 letters bequeathed to Mr Sitwell, I have omitted twenty-eight brief notes of no value, and one short letter which consists only of damaging and probably unjustified accusations against a business firm still in existence. The rest have been printed in their entirety: nothing has been omitted, and where dots occur they are George Moore's own. I have also included the two letters from Hone's *Life*: one from the original in the possession of Margherita Lady Howard de Walden, the other from Hone's printed text.

When he agreed that a selection of his letters to Edouard Dujardin should be translated by John Eglinton, Moore wrote to Dujardin on 21 November 1922: "Publish my letters if you like, but correct the mistakes." That injunction has been followed here, and with necessity, for George Moore never mastered the rudiments of spelling or punctuation. As he wrote to Edmund Gosse on 1 April 1917:

> Mine is a wandering mind, as I have said before, coming and going like a wind in and out of a field. At any moment I may forget how to spell the most ordinary word; very often it has befallen me to forget the spelling after having written the word quite correctly a few lines higher up the page. And with questions of grammar it is the same . . . Nature did not intend me for a scholar, that is certain.

Every effort has been made to render the letters intelligible and correct, though one or two proper names remain conjectural, and the author's system, or lack, of paragraphing has been preserved. For the convenience of readers, all French words, as well as titles of books and

18

newspapers, have been printed in italics, and the position of the address and date at the head of each letter has been standardised.

George Moore seldom dated his letters fully. In later years Lady Cunard kept the envelopes, and postmarks have been a great help, though several letters had clearly strayed into the wrong envelopes. I have been able to date all the remaining letters by internal or corroborative evidence, except for a dozen or so, which I have placed in what seem possible places. All dates within square brackets have been editorially supplied: every uncertain one is preceded by a question mark.

(7)

My first and greatest debt is to Mr Sacheverell Sitwell, the owner of the letters, and to Mr C. D. Medley, George Moore's literary executor and copyright-owner: without their co-operation this book could not have been published. I am also grateful to Mr Medley for permission to print extracts from Moore's books and letters to other people. Miss Nancy Cunard has helped me untiringly at every stage with information and encouragement. Other friends of Moore's who have most generously assisted me with facts, memories, and documents are Sir Thomas Beecham, Lady Juliet Duff, Mr Joseph Hone, Margherita Lady Howard de Walden, Mrs Mary Hutchinson, Mr W. K. Magee (John Eglinton), Mr Charles Morgan, Miss Athene Seyler, Loelia Duchess of Westminster, and Miss Elizabeth Williamson.

Two American scholars provided invaluable aid. Mr Edwin Gilcher, who has for twenty years been working on the authoritative bibliography of George Moore's writings, has most unselfishly placed his vast store of knowledge at my disposal, and Mr Charles Burkhart allowed me to use his unpublished thesis on Moore's letters to Edmund Gosse, W. B. Yeats, Mary Hutchinson, R. I. Best, and Nancy Cunard.

Many of the more recondite footnotes were kindly supplied by experts: notably the musical ones by Mr Ernest Bradbury of the *Yorkshire Post*, Mr Harold Rosenthal of the magazine *Opera*, and Mr David L. Webster of the Royal Opera House, Covent Garden. Two obscure French quotations were run to earth by brilliant pairs of researchers: one by Lady Diana Cooper and the Comtesse Jean de Polignac: the other by Professor Guy Chapman and Madame André Parreaux. For other help of great value I am indebted to Mr S. Allwood of the office of the Commissioners of Crown Lands, Lord Bridges, the Hon. Mrs Bryan Burns, Mr Martin Davies of the National Gallery, Mrs Alan Forster, Mr Richard Garnett, Professor Douglas Grant, Mr John Hayward, Mr David Hughes, Mr E. J. Mehew, Professor Sir John Neale, Mr Ernest Newman, Mr Ian Robertson of the Ashmolean Museum, Mrs Ruth Simon, the late Mr Allan Wade, Professor George Whalley, and Mr Kenneth Young.

For permission to include illustrations I have to thank Mr Cecil Beaton, Lady Beerbohm, Mr Alvin Langdon Coburn, Lady Diana Cooper, Mrs Kit Nicoll, Lord Sempill, Mr Myles Tonks, R.I., R.B.A., and Miss Elizabeth Williamson. I have been able to quote A.E.'s poem "A Farewell" through the kindness of the poet's son, Mr Diarmuid Russell, and of Messrs Macmillan & Co. Ltd.

Lastly, I owe a great debt of gratitude to Joseph Hone's *Life of George Moore* (1935), to the published volumes of Moore's Letters to Dujardin and Eglinton, and to Nancy Cunard's *G.M.: Memories of George Moore* (1956).

May 1957   RUPERT HART-DAVIS

20

[*14 May 1895*]   *Hotel Continental*
                                              Paris

You should not think that I do not want to see you
because I do not always answer your letters by return of
post. Sometimes one may be prevented from answering
a letter by return of post. Moreover you said that you
were coming to town on the 20th. You said nothing
about coming before. But I am sorry you did not receive
two letters which I addressed to America.[1] I hope they
will be forwarded. I sent you a bottle of scent—I was
buying some this morning and thought of you. Would
you care for a yard of scented flannel to put with your
things? It scents underwear beautifully. I do not know if
you know the flannel I mean—it is not sold in England.
It is specially prepared and keeps its odour six months or
more. The weather is very hot—unbearable. I saw
Huysmans[2] this morning and have arranged to hear
benediction with him—the Benedictine nuns who sing
Plain Chant. Last night I was at the first performance of
the *Tannhäuser*.[3] You know how I used to run down this
opera. Well, I have changed my opinion, somewhat.
There are some beautiful inspirations, and now I feel
inspiration before beautiful writing. When a man knows

[1] Where she had been married on 17 April.

[2] Joris-Karl Huysmans (1848–1907), the French novelist, had worked
his way through realism, symbolism and diabolism before, in his
novel *En Route* (1895), he turned finally to Catholicism.

[3] The "Paris version" of *Tannhäuser* was revived at the Opéra in
Paris on 13 May 1895 after an interval of thirty-four years. Another
company played it at Covent Garden in July, and G.M. wrote of this
performance in the *Speaker* of 20 July, comparing it unfavourably
with the Paris performance in May.

how to write he does not write so well—inspiration is lost in artistry. If it were not for *le concours* in the second act, the second act would be very fine. Even the duet which used to bore me seemed last night beautiful and true—the form is Italian but what matter—inspiration is after all the first thing. They of course played the version which Wagner rewrote after twenty years. He rewrote the Venus scene in the first act. You know that, but this you probably don't know, that he turned to the overture for some of the motives. He took the well-known air that comes into the Venus music—the overture Venus music—and developed it, making a beautiful thing out of a poor thing. You know the little air I mean. *Enfin.* . . . But why do I write all these things? Force of habit I suppose.

Always yours George Moore

14 December 1896   *92 Victoria Street*[1]

I am going North on Wednesday to hunt and shall be away for about a month. So I hope you will not come to London before Christmas as I should not like to miss you. I am very interested in your desire to write; you can think and there is but a step between thinking and writing. I remember many of your aphorisms and pithy phrases. You know that I always thought you were a clever woman, only at that moment you were on the crest of the wave of an exuberant youthfulness, but you always kept an evasive eye on the intellectual side of things. I don't expect to find you changed; we do not change; we develop; I am just what I was at twenty. I am going away hunting and my eagerness is the same . . . No, you will not change—*we* do not change. Do not be afraid to send me specimens of your writing, and remember that

[1] G.M. lived in a flat at this address from 1896 to 1901.

perseverance is essential. I must send you a book I have been reading with great interest, *Le Trésor des Humbles*.[1] If you wish to write, address to Selaby, Gainford, Darlington.[2]

Always yours George Moore

I have said nothing about your riding. I wonder—your nerve, how is it? Do write.

10 September [*1897*] *"Nuit de Septembre"*[3]

In your letter, dated the ninth, which I received this evening you say that you wrote to the Continental. No letter was forwarded though I left instructions. I have just telegraphed to enquire. Yesterday morning a feeling came over me that I should hear from you. You were then writing or thinking about writing. You speak about *The Triumph of Death* by d'Annunzio; I have just finished *L'Intrus*, another book by him.[4] I think it quite wonderful. You know that I seldom praise a novel—well, I could write twenty pages about *L'Intrus*. He writes as

[1] A book of essays by Maurice Maeterlinck (1896).

[2] The home of Mr and Mrs Charles Hunter. He was a wealthy coal-owner, and his wife Mary (1857–1931) an elder sister of Dame Ethel Smyth, the composer. In 1910 the Hunters moved to Hill Hall, near Epping, which had belonged to the Smyth family since the sixteenth century. Here Mrs Hunter entertained constantly: G.M., Henry James, Rodin, and other writers and artists were constant visitors. Mrs Hunter was a particular friend of J. S. Sargent, who painted several portraits of her and her daughters. It was Mary Hunter's gift of a bible to G.M. that began his interest in Jesus and Paul, and both *The Apostle* (1911) and *The Brook Kerith* (1916) were dedicated to her in gratitude.

[3] In 1894 G.M. had revised one of his early poems, giving it the new title of "Nuit de Septembre." It so appeared in all editions of *Confessions of a Young Man* from 1904.

[4] A French translation (1893) of d'Annunzio's novel *L'Innocente* (1891). *Il Trionfo della Morte* (1894) was published in French in 1896.

that fellow whose name begins with P and whose hair is red plays the piano.[1] In him we get the psychological novel; literature has apparently returned to *Clarissa Harlowe* and *La Princesse de Clèves*. He is a little wanting in outline—but what wonderful writing! Why are we always thinking about the same things at the same moment? . . . I had thought of sending you *L'Intrus* but, in the last letter I had from you, you said I had better not write until I heard from you. You said that you were going abroad and would write to me from abroad. If you had asked me to wait in Paris I should have waited. In your last letter you denied knowledge of a typewritten letter which someone wrote me. Do you remember? That was the last. It is most strange, for I wrote to the hotel for some clothes which had not come home from the wash when I left. These they sent me but no letter.

I read d'Annunzio in French. The French translation is wonderful, the best translation I ever read. It is at least equal to the original.

As ever George Moore

But when shall I see you? All this writing is vain if I am not to see you.

Friday night [*October 1897*]   *92 Victoria Street*

If you have *Le Triomphe de la Mort* you might send it to me. I will write and tell you how it strikes me. I've just come home from dinner at Henry Russell's—the singing master.[2] I know no house where one spends such pleasant evenings. His brother is an extraordinary pianist. He

---

[1] Ignacy Jan Paderewski (1860-1941).

[2] Henry Russell (1813–1900), besides teaching singing, wrote more than eight hundred songs, including "Cheer, Boys, Cheer" and "A Life on the Ocean Wave". He was the father of Sir Landon Ronald (1873-1938), the composer and conductor.

played the overture to the *Meistersinger*, the prelude to *Tristan*, the overture and new ballet music [from] *Tannhäuser* and the *Liebestod, Tristan*. What a delight a musical evening is! One feels so clean and refreshed after it. He played the third act or nearly of the *Valkyrie*. Musical society interests me most now. One feels so happy and content after music. Do you know the plaint of the sirens in the new *Tannhäuser* music?—the music he wrote for Paris. Their cry is like the cry of the earth itself, of the water, an elemental cry for life or of regret for life. In little bits, often not more than a bar, Wagner tells the deepest secrets. This is one of the secrets of life, her most hidden secret; it is in our hearts, but beyond words.

Yours ever George Moore

If you'd like the music I'd send it.

[*late October 1897*][1]   *92 Victoria Street*

Thank you for the book, which I shall not however be able to read for some time, for I am reading *Le Triomphe de la Mort* and I read very slowly. I cannot read a book in less than eight or ten days. I read a chapter a day and I assimilate it like a cow in torpid silence. Are you coming to London before Christmas? If you are I'll wait, if you are not I'll write—a matter of music connected with my book. There is no news and there is a great deal of a sort— I am going to the Richter concert on Monday and expect to be delighted; the programme is most interesting. By the way, can you play the ballet music; it is very very

[1] On 3 November 1897 G.M. wrote to Dujardin: "Read *The Triumph of Death*—I am half way through it." The last of the series of Richter concerts at the Queen's Hall (a Wagner programme) took place on Monday, 1 November. I have dated this letter, and the two preceding ones, accordingly.

difficult, but is not the plaint of the sirens pathetic? Pathetic because all love cries are. Though we do not know it, they are cries of the will to live—the future generation that does not wish to be called into being. It is these remote feelings that music, the most remote of all the arts, expresses so well.

Very sincerely George Moore

10 February 1898   *92 Victoria Street*

I felt too discouraged to write. There is no use in explaining further, you know very well. I have almost ceased to believe that I shall ever see you again. I am going to Paris in a few days, some day at the end of next week, and shall be away for about three weeks. I want to get away somewhere, anywhere where I shall not have to write. *Evelyn Innes* is being printed but I am still writing it. But the book entitled *Evelyn Innes* is only half the book originally intended. The subject proved too vast to be treated in one book. I had to break it off in the middle; the next book will be called *Sister Teresa*. *Evelyn Innes* will be published here and in America some time in April.

The lady you mention in your letter is a friend of mine. She is agreeable and pleasant but she does not attract me any further and so far as I know she is as satisfied with our present relations as I am. Last night I dined with Harry Lynch[1] but there were a number of people there and your name was only mentioned. He said he had heard of you through his Cambridge friend who had been stopping at Holt. D'Annunzio's book *Les Vierges aux Rochers* I did not finish. It did not seem to me nearly so good as the others. He is a wonderful writer

[1] Henry Finnis Blosse Lynch (1862-1913), traveller and author, came from a County Mayo family. He climbed Mount Ararat in 1893 and was Liberal M.P. for Ripon 1906-10.

and he has interesting things to say, but he has no power for the massing and the ordination of events, I add for the symbolisation of events. I don't know if you will understand this last phrase; it requires explanation but it would take too long to explain; *une lettre n'est pas un cours de littérature.* My publisher and his readers think that *Evelyn Innes* is my best book. They promise a great deal but I no longer pay heed to promises.

I will send you back d'Annunzio's book. Thank you for lending it.

Always yours George Moore

[*September 1898*]
Airlie Castle
Alyth
N.B.

You hear everything and I wonder how you could have heard that I was going to the Mintos'. My visit was a pleasant one—you know I am not a success in country houses, but not only the last but the present visit is most pleasant. Lady Airlie (the dowager) is a woman whose beauty of mind is an enchantment; I know no one more noble. But as you don't know her there is no use my describing her. I am very friendly with Lady Minto; I like her and hope to retain her friendship. We went for some drives and she talked at length and I seem to know her better. But now she is going away to Canada for five years, so there is an end to that.[1] Lady Randolph[2] was there and Lord and Lady Essex, Lady Lister-Kaye, the Duke d'Alba and Mr and Mrs Maguire. Mrs Maguire (Julia) is

---

[1] The fourth Earl of Minto (1847–1914) was Governor-General of Canada 1898–1904 and Viceroy of India 1905–10. He married Mary, daughter of General the Hon. Charles Grey.

[2] Jennie Jerome (1854–1921) married (1874) Lord Randolph Spencer Churchill, third son of the seventh Duke of Marlborough, and was the mother of Sir Winston.

very charming—the cleverest woman I have met since you.[1] I am going on to the Edens[2] for a few days. Then I go to Beckett's[3] for the Leeds Festival, and then I return to London to write *Sister Teresa*. All the winter I shall see no society whatever; society is a snare and he who gets entangled will never come to fruition. I have altered *Evelyn Innes* and enormously improved it—some of the alterations are in the second edition, but the more interesting alterations will not appear till the third edition. I will send you a copy, one of a dozen which I am having printed for myself. This little edition will be out next week.[4] Nothing in the world would induce me to lecture in New York. What do you take me for, a mummer? This letter is a failure, I cannot write tonight, my sentences jolt along like a market cart.

As ever George Moore

12 October [*1898*]   *92 Victoria Street*

I returned to London on Monday and your letter arrived on Tuesday. I don't think I could have had a pleasanter month, but I am glad to get back, for pleasure

[1] Julia Beatrice, wife of James Rochfort Maguire, daughter of the first Viscount Peel, granddaughter of Sir Robert, and close friend of Cecil Rhodes.

[2] Sir William Eden, the seventh Baronet (1849–1915), landowner, painter, eccentric, one-time friend of Whistler, and father of Sir Anthony, was a neighbour of the Hunters in Durham. G.M. often stayed with him and rode to hounds there.

[3] Ernest William Beckett (1856–1917), of the Yorkshire banking family. He was Conservative M.P. for Whitby from 1885 to 1905, when he succeeded his uncle as second Lord Grimthorpe.

[4] The first edition of *Evelyn Innes* was published by T. Fisher Unwin in June 1898, the second in August. This "little edition" of twelve copies was a trial third edition, consisting of copies of the second edition corrected by the pasting over of certain pages with proofs of a revised text. G.M. sent W. B. Yeats a copy on October 28.

is not life. I had hoped to begin writing today, but it will be some time before I succeed in getting back into my furrow. We both love amusement, it is very seductive but very unsatisfying. As for the news and gossip, that too is amusing but one cannot often write it: it loses its character when it is written down: ink is an adjuvant which develops a dangerous quality in harmless ingredients. Of course I met the usual round of people—Lady Randolph always interests me. Lady Algernon Lennox was at Kirkstall Grange (Ernest Beckett's) and I liked her too—but I cannot go with my preferences. I feel like an elephant trying to [*word missing*] the flowers. Besides what can it matter? A far deeper impression I got from a book called *On the Eve*, by Tourgueneff. I have never read anything so beautiful—I did not know that anything so perfect existed. One of the apostles has been here this morning; he is writing, it appears, about what other people think about Tolstoi. I found him most agreeable, not only because he came to hear me talk, but because he told me many interesting things about Tourgueneff. It appears that my opinion of *War and Peace* conforms exactly to Tourgueneff's—he, my interlocutor, is about to publish a letter by Tourgueneff in which the same opinion is expressed in the same words, at least so he tells me.[1] The Leeds Festival was very interesting and Palestrina was its success. Everyone was enchanted with his *Stabat Mater*.[2] But it seems as if I should never get back into my furrow—amusement is most demoralising. I use the word in the sense of disintegrating: I must strive to reintegrate myself. When

[1] This interview with an unnamed Russian visitor provided the material for chap. v of *Avowals* (1919).

[2] Palestrina's *Stabat Mater* was performed at the Leeds Festival on 6 October 1898, the day after the first performance of Elgar's *Caractacus*. Sir Arthur Sullivan was the conductor.

do you come to London? You will write I hope and let
me see you.

Always yours George Moore

I should like to go to Paris and see pictures with you,
but at the end of the visit I foresee much bitterness. Any
further bitterness might make me hate you and I don't
want to do that. But you must tell me if there is danger of
this. I have had a delightful bicycle tour. I visited all the
sacred places—places made sacred by memories and many
passings from the mortal into the immortal. I believe in
a sixth sense, the sense of place. The elder civilisations
were nearer the immortals than we are, I am sure of
that; and round these places they saw the immortals
ascending in circles of fire. So they built their altars there
and guarded the mysteries. The Druid crypt at New-
grange[1] is one of the most striking things the world has
to show. The passages are so narrow that one has to creep
on one's hands and knees, and they open into a small
chamber in which there is a vast sacrificial cup. The
enormous rocks which these great people piled together
are carved with the symbol of the sun [*rough drawing of
four concentric circles*]. The centre is the earth, the first
circle is the circle of the waters, the second the circle of
Tir-na-nogue, the third is the circle of the infinite Lir.
The days were beautifully fine and earth lay like a nun
breathless with adoration. Sitting on the hilltop seeing
the sunlight like a vast spiritual presence enfolding the
earth, I thought of the strange pagan spirituality which
accepted as a fundamental truth that man and nature are
one, moved by the same impulses. But have such thoughts

[1] Near Slane in County Meath, north of Dublin.

George Moore, by William Orpen, 1903

any interest for you, or are you absorbed by the triviali-
ties of the war in Africa, the open door in China and
grouse-shooting in Scotland? Sitting on that hilltop in
sight of Tara I saw Ireland through a haze of divinities.
I have nearly finished *Sister Teresa*—I have only to rewrite a few passages. *Grania*, which is you, is nearly done;
I shall finish it next week.[1] I have then to write a long
article for the *Nineteenth Century* on the revival of the
Irish language.[2] The language question interests me more
than anything else now. I often think of you amid my
many occupations, and the past though it recedes day by
day does not grow fainter. So it would not be well to
go to Paris to quarrel, and we might quarrel bitterly.

Always yours George Moore

6 October [*1904*]   *Kirkstall Grange*
Headingley
Leeds

Dearest Maud, dearest Primavera!

I do not know what primavera means, or if I have spelt
it sufficiently for you to recognise the word. It means
Spring, doesn't it? It means joy, the joy of green leaves

[1] *Diarmuid and Grania*, a play written in vexed collaboration between G.M. and W. B. Yeats, was produced by the F. R. Benson
company at the Gaiety Theatre, Dublin, on 21 October 1901.
Elgar, at G.M.'s request, contributed some incidental music (see
Salve, 1912, chap. vi). The only surviving typescript of the play,
corrected by both authors, was given or bequeathed by G.M. to
Lady Cunard, and it was this text that was finally published in the
Dublin Magazine for April-June 1951. I have dated this letter Autumn
1900, since it is known that the play was shown to Mrs Patrick
Campbell before the end of the year, though the bicycle tour which is
described in the letter and later formed the subject of chaps. ii and iii
of *Salve* is there dated 1901.

[2] This article, entitled "Plea for the Soul of the Irish People",
appeared in the *Nineteenth Century and After* for February 1901.

with the flutter of wings among the leaves. And you, dearest, mean all these things to me, for you are not, I am convinced, a mere passing woman but an incarnation of an idea—we are all types more or less defined, we all represent an idea, but you do more than faintly represent an idea. You are the idea. In you Nature has succeeded in expressing herself and completely. We perforce make, if we would make them at all, poems out of words or musical notes or chalk lines or pigments. You take yourself and make a poem out of your body and out of your spirit. You are at once the poet and the poem, and you create yourself not with silks and pearls, though these things are beautiful upon you, but by your intense desire of beauty and life. I am thinking of you, that goes without saying, but today I am wondering what you would think of Strauss. The Festival has been going on for three days but today is the first musical impression I received.[1] He captured me at once just as Whitman did and much in the same way, by telling me about life, telling me interesting things about life. Brahms bores me. Brahms I am convinced *n'est pas grand-chose*—he has thought and read and his writing is full of happy turns of expression, but what are happy turns of expression to me, when behind them there is no irresistible fountain of life? There is no fountain in Brahms, no spring of enchanted life, bubbling, singing, creating a green spring tide. In simple words Brahms is a pedant no better than Tennyson. The miserable Poet Laureate[2] is here and he asked me if I didn't prefer Brahms to Strauss. I said I would as soon

[1] Richard Strauss's tone poem *Tod und Verklärung* was performed at the Leeds Festival on 6 October 1904. The conductor was Sir Charles Stanford. Brahms's Violin Concerto had been played by Kreisler on 5 October.

[2] Alfred Austin (1835–1913) had succeeded Tennyson as Poet Laureate in 1896, after a four-year interregnum.

read—the poor little wretch thought I was going to say "you". I said "your predecessor". Dear Maud, write to me about your mother and look into your affairs; if you do not apply yourself to understanding your affairs I am afraid that your money will melt away.

Always affectionately yours George Moore

Sir Hedworth Williamson is here. I like him very much—he is really very intelligent.[1]

Sunday [October 1904]   *4 Upper Ely Place*
                                                            Dublin[2]
Dearest Primavera,

I spent Saturday finishing my comedy[3] and when it was finished—now it *is* finished—I was too tired to write. For this I was truly sorry—I didn't like to miss the mail. I know that you like to get a letter from me. As I write these lines you are steaming into New York harbour. Dear Primavera, I had a lovely time this summer—why is it that fate is so kind?—fate isn't kind to other men. Few men have known all pleasure of spirit and sense, and I knew them all this summer—the summer that is gone, that has just fallen behind us. But you would much sooner that I wrote you news and it is only natural that you should. But what news have I to write? Hedworth

[1] Ninth Baronet (1867–1942).

[2] G.M.'s home from 1901 to 1911.

[3] This play had a long history. It was originally written by G.M. in collaboration with Mrs Pearl Craigie and called *The Peacock's Feathers*, but after her death in 1906 G.M. rewrote it as *Elizabeth Cooper*, and the Stage Society produced it in London on 23 June 1913, in which year it was published. G.M. was much annoyed by the production at the Comédie Royale, Paris, in 1914 of a French version by Edouard Dujardin entitled *Clara Florise*, though he had in fact authorised the arrangement. Eventually G.M. rewrote the play yet again as *The Coming of Gabrielle*. This version was published in 1920 and produced for three matinées at the St James's Theatre in July 1923, with Athene Seyler in the leading part (see pp. 67 and 126).

Williamson grew a little tiresome, his continuous singing and dancing got on Colonel Collins' nerves. The Colonel used to fly from the drawing room cursing Hedworth and very appreciative of the joke that Hedworth was a little more than a lady and not quite a gentleman. Miss Fairfax was there,[1] a very beautiful and interesting girl. I wonder if she loves Ernest and if he will marry her. Ernest's daughters have grown up very nice intelligent young women. The little Laureate was there; he was pleasanter than Mallock—everyone is beginning to find Mallock a bore.[2] The Laureate is seventy and it is difficult for a man of seventy not to look out of place in one of Ernest's virgin parties. Minnie Paget[3] I saw once again, she sent for me; I am obliged to you for the introduction, for I think I shall always see her with pleasure; she is of our kin and one must keep to one's kin. The question now is whether I shall take a flat in London or in Paris—I think I shall have money to do either. Bourchier[4] has definitely accepted our terms and the agreement will be signed in a few days. I heard from Pearl last night and I read the play to three or four friends who came to dine and to hear it— they were delighted; I only intended to read one act but they insisted on hearing the three and I could see that they thought the comedy one of the best of modern times. My own opinion interested me more than theirs did, for I'm very sensitive and if a thing bores me I cannot go on reading. Gretel[5] was alive like a horse under me all the

[1] At Ernest Beckett's house, Kirkstall Grange. See previous letter.
[2] W. H. Mallock (1849–1923), author of *The New Republic* (1877) and many other books.
[3] Born an American, Mary Paran Stevens, she married General Sir Arthur Paget (1851–1928) and became a society hostess in London. She died in 1919.
[4] Arthur Bourchier (1863–1927) was one of many actor-managers who failed to produce G.M.'s comedy.
[5] I cannot vouch for or explain this word.

time, losing no jot of muscular strength till the goal was reached. The comedy if it is a great success will be my ransom—the comedy will give me my Primavera. But you must look into your money affairs; somehow I feel that your mother's affairs require looking into, you should if you can apply yourself to them; money runs away very easily and I heard your mother say that she hadn't done a "thing right since Fred's death."[1] A wrong current will sweep away the biggest fortune. I shall be glad indeed to have news of your mother. Mrs Campbell is anxious to take your mother to the south of Europe—you will have seen her before you get this letter. I told her that I should like to meet you in the south of Europe, anywhere. Your mother, Mrs Campbell, you and I. I cannot think of your mother's kindness to me without experiencing a sudden access of tenderness. I am swept away and I do not know which sentiment prevails, affection, gratitude or admiration. Give your mother my best love, tell her that I look forward to seeing her. I can conceive no greater pleasure unless seeing you; and I have come to associate you two so intimately in my thoughts that one without the other would not be sufficient.

As ever, dearest Primavera, George Moore

22 *October* [*1904*]   *4 Upper Ely Place*
                                                                   Dublin

Dearest Maud,

I have just written to your mother and a good deal of what I said to her I might repeat here—the memory of those grey moonlights and that green valley will never be forgotten. I remember the trees, their shape, how the shepherd sat under one—his flock about him—and how the line of the hillside dipped. There is no part of the

---

[1] Lady Cunard's mother was now Mrs Frederick Tichenor.

house[1] I do not remember, because you were there with me unpacking furniture, hanging pictures, and I remember the chestnut trees at the back, Nancy and her governess, and the long roads, a little bare and dreary, that flow on over the hills—far away. But above all these things I remember your mien and motion, your brightly coloured cheeks, your fair hair, fair as the hair in an eighteenth-century pastel, and your marble eyes (my pen is a bad one and will not write at all). How I live on memories of Maud. Sometimes I think I only do things in order that I may brood upon them. In this I have changed very little. Do you remember? . . . But you would like news much better than memories. What news have I? I am trying to finish *The Lake* and am experiencing the greatest difficulty in writing the end. This story is as difficult to write as *Sister Teresa*. Thank you for your offer to dispose of the play. I doubt if it is possible to dispose of it in America until it has been produced in London. Moreover I am only part owner and have no authority.

Dearest, always affectionately yours George Moore

Wednesday 25 January [*1905*]   *4 Upper Ely Place*
                                                                    Dublin

Dearest Maud,

I have just received your sad letter[2] and I have sent you a wire saying that I wrote last Saturday to 100 East 17th Street. I hope you will get the letter before you leave. Letters take longer than one thinks—yours was dated 15th and it was not delivered till today. I was very fond of your dear mother, as I might well be, for she was an angel to me always—she wanted us to be friends, and I

[1] Nevill Holt.
[2] Lady Cunard's mother, Mrs Tichenor, had recently died in America.

am sure she will be disappointed, if her spirit survives, if any estrangement happened. But we cannot be estranged —an estrangement between us would be almost as unnatural as an estrangement between you and her. I look forward to seeing you. Send me a wire and I'll meet you at Cork.

As ever, dearest, George Moore

Thursday [*26 January 1905*]   *4 Upper Ely Place*
                                                   Dublin

Your letter arrived here last night and I answer it at once, though there will not be a mail before Saturday. I must write my letter for I can think of nothing but your dear mother. There was a bond of sympathy between us three. I don't know if you and she were as sensible to it as I was—I suppose you must have been. Your mother never tried to come between you and me; instinct seems to have told her that we were destined to be friends for life, and she knew that such predestined friendships must follow their own courses. She was so much occupied with her own husband that I never really knew her till he died —till last summer, thrice happy summertime for ever rememberable by me. It was last August that I began to love her—there is no other word, for all affection is love; and I began to see you in her; and her love for you and her appreciation of you endeared her to me. You say that she was devoted to me! That happy happy summertime —was god or mortal ever favoured as I was, living between you two women for one whole month in that beautiful house overlooking the wide terrace. I remember the balustrade and the mysterious green land beyond it flowing away, dipping; and the valley stretching for miles and miles—the hillside opposite with its long woods and the house which King John once lived in—Rockingham.

My room is well remembered—the oak passage outside and the beautiful eastern rugs that your mother brought from America. Do you remember that sunny afternoon in June when we unpacked her innumerable boxes and found jam-pots and chintz curtains, fish-hooks and suede gloves, fire-irons and fiddles? Do you remember our laughter? That part of our life is over and done—how intensely one remembers—my room hung with Italian engravings, and the round table at which I used to sit writing, and your ringing voice calling me away, or your mother's, or dear Nancy's—those green swards! The ash tree within whose circular shade the shepherd and his flock used to gather—"a Leicestershire Abraham" I used to say, for life changes little in essentials. Dearest Maud, you are all I have, it is through you that I know that I am alive. There was a bond of sympathy between us three . . . Yes there was. Your mother thought of you as I think of you—hardly as a human being; you always seemed to us more like a fairy, a sprite—Abraham reappears in the Leicestershire shepherd and you represent some dream, heroism or beauty, one of those everlasting states of consciousness which do not die with the individual but pass on from generation to generation, a beauty that never perishes, a fire that never wanes. Your mother always thought of you as Primavera—the idea is as much hers as mine. Dearest Primavera, it is sad to think that your mother has gone—only you and I really mourn her; who else understands as we understand? All the love I had for giving I have given you. My heart is overflowing—I must stop writing. I cannot think today, I can only feel. When shall I see you? Shall I come to Cork or will you come to Dublin and see your pictures
and yours ever George Moore

Whatever else may happen Rodin has certainly spent an afternoon hearing of your charms. The price of a marble bust is 1000 and you can have a bronze cast of any one of the many beautiful things in his studio for about a couple of hundred. Rodin is a man of sixty-five, so I would advise you to get the bust done this summer. There will always be motor cars and hunters, but when Rodin's hand begins to fail and his eye begins to see less clearly there will be no more sculpture. The opinion of every artist is that no sculpture has been done since antiquity that for beauty of execution can compare with Rodin's. I know little of sculpture but I am sure that no greater bust than Hugo has been done since antiquity. Some think that what he does now is better than what he used to do. I don't. I would remind you that motor cars and hunters are passing things and drop into wreckage: but a bust outlasts Rome. Please let me know if you will pay 200 for a bronze. Would you like a sensuality or an austerity? I met Heinemann and he is going to publish *The Lake*.[1] We dined with two women friends of his, in a café, and went to the theatre afterwards. I am sending you a book—*une lecture délicieuse mais difficile*.

                                        As ever George Moore

Rodin is going to Scotland in August to do Balfour's bust,[2] so if you want to see him, and I suppose you do,

---

[1] Rodin was born in 1840, and Heinemann published *The Lake* in November 1905. I have dated this letter accordingly.

[2] Neither the Balfour family nor the Musée Rodin has any knowledge of the existence of such a bust.

you had better come to Paris at the beginning of August. Rodin does not know for certain if he is going at the beginning or at the end of the month—I fancy it will be at the end—Parliament sits till the 10th generally.

As ever George Moore

I did not send you the *Confessions* because I am waiting for the Tauchnitz edition.[1] The English edition is detestable—thoroughly detestable. I have written to Leipzig to ask if they will print a few copies on Holland paper (I suppose I should say Dutch paper). The ordinary edition will arrive here on Wednesday or Thursday—you shall have your copy on Friday.

13 July 1905   *Imperial Hotel*
                                                        Castlebar

How many years ago is it since I wrote some French verses for you? I remember saying that you would never find another Englishman to write French verses for you. And today I say you will never get a letter from another sent from the above address. No one will ever write to you from the Imperial Hotel Castlebar but I. I like to be exceptional even in little things, and I like to confer favours on Castlebar. I have just put aside Wagner's letters to Mathilde.[2] They roll on seemingly for ever yet without wearying one. I wonder what one would think of them if the author were not Wagner. Was there ever so garrulous a man? Was there ever a man so interested in himself? Well, he had the right to be, for he was the most interesting thing alive and he clearly knew it; and

[1] Published 1905. No copies on Holland paper are known to G.M.'s bibliographer. The "English edition" was a squat volume printed on featherweight paper and published by Werner Laurie.

[2] *Richard Wagner to Mathilde Wesendonck*, translated by William Ashton Ellis (1905). See *Vale* (1914), chap. vii.

July 18th 1905

How many years ago is absence I wrote some
French verses for you? I remember saying
that you would never find another english
man to write French verses for you. And
today I say you will never get ~~another~~ a letter from another
~~English~~ to the above address; No one will ever write
to you from the Imperial hotel Castlebar
but I. I like to be exceptional even in little
things, and I like to confer favours on Castlebar
I have just put aside Wagner's letters to Mathilde
the roll on seemingly forever yet without
wearying one. I wonder what one would
think of them if the author were not Wagner
Was there ever so garrulous a man?
Was there ever a man so interested in himself, well, he had the right to be for he was
the most interesting thing alive and he
clearly knew it; and egotism is the food that
inspires the letter writer and good letters
are all about the letter writer. And if I were
a letter writer I should tell you how it
bores me to come here, and dine with
judges and drive, to more than, with my brother who

egotism is the god that inspires the letter-writer and good letters are all about the letter-writer. And if I were a letter-writer I should tell you how it worries me to come here and dine with judges[1] and drive to Moore Hall with my brother who dearly loves the Georgian house on the hilltop. I should tell you about *The Lake*, tell you that I fear I shall never be able to write the book at all, and I should copy pieces from the proofs, and the following day I should write telling you that I had received some rusks which when dipped into hot milk inspire the dull lagging brains of authors. But I am not sufficiently interested in any of these details of my daily life to write them. It would interest me much more for me to find expression for my feelings for you, were I able to find expression for them. I should like to express my gratitude to you for the extraordinary kindness and sympathy you give me. Other women have wished to be kind to me, but I did not want their kindness and tried to escape from it; but your kindness delights me—it does far more than delight me, it fills me with wonder and with a double wonder. I wonder what god selected me for happiness and why he selected me. For I am the most fortunate of men; surely the most fortunate man in the world is he who meets a woman who enchants him as a work of art enchants. I find in you Manet, Berthe Morisot, Tourgueneff, Balzac, Shelley, and the works I cannot write but would, were I the George Moore that George Moore sees in front of him, beguiling him, luring him like a will-o'-the-wisp. If I have failed to write what I dreamed I might write, one thing I have not failed in—you. You are at once the vase and the wine in the vase. You are the music and the instrument which produces the music, and you are a prodigious virtuoso, and while thinking of you one thinks of all that one loves most intimately. I said to

[1] In 1905 G.M. was High Sheriff of County Mayo.

41

Howard,[1] 'She is like music, like Wagner's music', and he said 'No, not a bit like Wagner's music'. 'You are quite right', I answered, 'she is more like Mozart. The Symphony in G Major. She is as joyous as it.' Howard didn't know the G Major Symphony or he thought my remark foolish. Very likely I am foolish but I am less foolish than many another, for I am wise enough to delight in my folly and to take pride in it. You are my folly, and what an exquisite folly, and how happy I am in my folly and how I marvel at it! For very few men have seen their ideal as close to them and as clearly as I have seen mine. Very few have possessed all they were capable of desiring of beauty and grace; I have possessed more, for the reality has exceeded the desire. You seem to me as marvellous as a rose, as a tea rose in its prime, as Shelley's hymn to Pan, as a bust by a Greek or Florentine sculptor. A sky full of stars does not astonish me more than your face, your marmoreal eyes. 'Time cannot wither nor custom stale', and for twelve years the wonder has never grown less. A man said yesterday, 'None has enjoyed life as much as you, for you relive your life again and again in memory.' *Et c'est vrai, j'ai le culte du souvenir*, and for weeks and months, for years I shall remember how you came down to Seaford House[2] in your electric brougham. That vehicle is for ever enshrined in my memory. You can never—and for this I pity you—you can never form an idea of the wonder it is to me to see you—to think you and dream you. I do not know if it be the eternal idea of

[1] The Rt Hon Thomas Evelyn Scott-Ellis, eighth Baron Howard de Walden (1880–1946), succeeded his father in 1899. He was a wealthy man and an untiring patron of the arts. In particular he subsidised Herbert Trench's season at the Haymarket Theatre in 1909, at which *King Lear* and Maeterlinck's *Blue Bird* were produced. He was also a supporter of the composer Josef Holbrooke, for whose operas *Dylan* and *The Children of Don* he supplied the libretti.

[2] Lord Howard de Walden's London house in Belgrave Square.

joy which you represent on earth, or its outward form that delights me most—the gold of your hair, your hand like a spray of fern. You come into a room filling the air with unpremeditated music. The best comparison I can think of is the indefinite hum of a fountain and its various colour transformations—you are as unreal as a fountain and as spiritual. The water surges compelled by a force unknown and we are cooled, refreshed, soothed and charmed; the water falls back full of fleeting iridescent colour. Would that I could restrain my pen, for you will not be won by exaltations. But I cannot keep myself from thanking you for your kindness; I want you to know that I am grateful; it would be terrible if I did not appreciate—I mean if you did not feel that I understood. I must praise, for it is a pleasure to praise, and he who is happy must speak his happiness even though he loses it by speech. The loss of happiness through speech is one of the oldest stories in the world. Prudence tells me I would do well to tear up this letter but I cannot listen to the voice of Prudence.

As ever yours George Moore

I have just read Mathilde's letters and I have read them with tears in my eyes. Sorrow is more beautiful than happiness, more wistful and much deeper, and in these letters one perceives the depth of the relation that may exist between men and women—in a word these letters tell us again that love of man for woman (better still the love of woman for man) is the most beautiful thing in the world.

16 July [*1905*]   *Rossmally*
Westport
Ireland

I am here till tomorrow, staying with my agent who is likewise my sub-sheriff. Now will you do something for

me, will you ask Pansy[1] to do something for me? A
head of you for preference ... A slight thing; I don't want
her to finish it; pastel or oils, whichever medium she likes
—not a pastel all worked up to look like an oil. Do this
and write to me. I sent you a long letter from Castlebar.

Always yours George Moore

Sunday [August 1905]   *Le Val Changis*
                                          Avon
                                          Fontainebleau

I am here with my old friend Dujardin[2] and last night
we sat up till one o'clock rearranging a comedy which he
is writing. And the same evening has happened before
and will happen again and again. Life is but an eternal
recurrence, and it is well that it should be so, for I look
forward to seeing you in Holt again, and I look forward
after my death to meeting you again in Holt: a billion
years hence Harry Lynch and I will sit talking about you
in the great hall in front of the tapestries. And in this
sweet faith I wish to live and die. Yesterday I bought a
picture, a beautiful thing by Madame Morisot that will
enchant me when I return to Dublin. I saw some beautiful
pictures and I thought it a pity that you do not spend some
of your money on pictures instead of spending it all on
motor cars and servants' wages. The admirable James by
the way forgot to pack up a shirt, and shirts cost 7/6d

[1] Mrs Pansy Cotton, an American, painted a large portrait of Lady
Cunard.

[2] Edouard Dujardin (1861-1949) in the eighties founded the *Revue
Wagnérienne*, the *Revue Indépendente*, and the *Revue des Idées*. His
Les Lauriers sont Coupés (1887) was the first stream-of-consciousness
novel and influenced James Joyce. In the nineties Dujardin wrote
three symbolist tragedies in blank verse. He then turned biblical
exegetist and his *La Source du Fleuve Chrétien* (1906) was partly responsible for G.M.'s biblical researches. See *Ave* (1911), pp. 63–64.

apiece. Will you ask him to send it to Dublin. This morning I lay in bed till eleven thinking of a dedication for *The Lake* and I got out of bed and wrote a page that suddenly came into my mind. I will send it to you in a few days when I have gone over it and if it pleases me a little bit. But I doubt if *The Lake* is worthy of your acceptance.[1] On Wednesday or Thursday I shall go and see Monet and I hope to get a picture from him. How that is to be done I don't know, for I have spent all my spare cash on Berthe Morisot. I found an old photograph of myself here this morning, taken at the time when I met you on "life's rough way" and strayed down "the primrose path" that leads to everlasting memory. I wonder if you would like to have it; I am afraid to send it. But will you send me the notes that follow Verlaine's lovely lines, *Mon coeur est un lac.* A couple of bars will do, for it is with these notes that I begin the dedication. But is the book worthy of your acceptance? I am not sure, and I have no confidence in any opinion but yours, and I am thinking of sending you the typewritten copy, but you are too busy just now—you will be able to judge it better in proof. Then it will be too late to withdraw the book if it doesn't meet your approval. There is some pretty landscape in the book—it is my landscape book—and some of the landscape is a memory of the forest. "The forest is like a harp", the breeze lifts the branches and a bird sings: a touch of art was added to the vague murmur I hear and the Siegfried music was made. Why do you never go to France; the beautiful French country is entrancing; it is to me; home does not stir me. I am

[1] Probably Lady Cunard thought not, for when *The Lake* appeared it carried a two-page dedication to Edouard Dujardin, written in French and dated 17 August 1905. G.M. persistently tried to dedicate his books to Lady Cunard, but it was many years before she agreed (see pp. 96-97, 107-111 and 140).

sure that my love of France is like Christ's love of Mary and my love of England is like Christ's love of Martha.

As ever George Moore

Saturday [August–September 1905]   *Hotel Continental*
Paris

You do not say what the operation is for. How extraordinary disease is. I thought you were the last person who would require an operation. Do write and say what the operation is for. The proofs I cannot send you—I rewrite the book on the proof sheets. My books begin to exist when the revise comes in. The musical phrase that you like goes to Verlaine's beautiful poem:

Ton âme est un lac d'amour
Dont mes désirs sont les cygnes.[1]

As ever George Moore

27 October [1905]   *4 Upper Ely Place*
Dublin

At last, at last. I sent you the drawing because it seems to me not to be without merit and because I might send letters by the dozen without getting an answer. I sent a letter with the drawing but I gather that you did not get that letter or have forgotten it. I am not blaming you for not writing, why should you write? I write to no one; all or nearly all the letters I receive remain unanswered. *The Lake* will not be published till the 10th of November

[1] In *Memoirs of my Dead Life* (1906) G.M. quoted these lines again (with *pensées* instead of *désirs*) and commented: "For a long time I thought these verses were Verlaine's, but they are much less original." They were in fact written by Armand Renaud, in a poem called "Les Cygnes", and set to music by Reynaldo Hahn.

46

on account of the American edition. If you don't like it you will like the book I have just finished, *Moods and Memories*. Or would you like better *Memoirs of my Dead Life?*[1] I am not sure that *Memoirs of my Dead Life* doesn't sound like the autobiography of an eighteenth-century lady's maid. How is Emma?

Now about London. I should like to go to London later, about Christmas. But you will not be in London then, and London without seeing you will not be London. Not for me at least. The end of the month would suit me better than the beginning. If I am to get through my work I must work for shifts of three months. But I must see you, for you are the light—you make me feel that I am alive, and life is what we are all after. You are the light, I am but an accumulator and my supply is running low. Just tell me what you would like me to do.

As ever George Moore

9 *January 1906*   4 *Upper Ely Place*
                                              Dublin

My dear,

I write to you because I am thinking of you. As I sit by the fire I seem to see you like a star in a dark sky—my star, that one which I must for ever follow. No man has absorbed you as you have absorbed me and I am sorry, for it must be lonely to live in the dark, to see no star ahead of one. Other men have wives, children, religion, god. I have my star, an ideal, my ideal of light, loveliness and grace which I follow always and which I shall see shining when my eyes grow dim and the spectacle is about to fade out of them for ever. I am writing the Avignon episode, for it served to show me how inveter-

[1] "*Un joli titre pour des souvenirs publiés de son vivant:* SOUVENIRS DE MA VIE MORTE" (*Journal des Frères Goncourt*, 28 May 1857).

47

ate my admiration and my love of you are.[1] They are as inherent, as much part of me, as Ingres, Manet, Shelley, Balzac or Tourgueneff—more than they. When I have written this story in your honour I am going to write a pamphlet entitled *Fairwell*[2]; it will I think make a noise in the world. But I care very little whether it does or doesn't . . . I am thinking now of those days at Holt when your mother's boxes arrived and we unpacked them together. The pretty May sunlight was dancing in the trees, and along the grass "the lilacs bloomed in the courtyard," and that reminds me of—not the variorum edition of Whitman but the edition of Poe which you sent me and which I cannot lay my hands on. Your dear mother we shall never see again! How strange it seems, and in the three weeks I spent at Holt I seemed to have learnt to know her so well, better possibly than I know anything else. I suppose that is why I think about her so much. You are a hard woman in many ways, but if you were less hard I don't think you would have held me captive such a long time; I do not complain of my captivity—good heavens no; it is the only allegiance I acknowledge, and man without an allegiance is like a ball of thistledown. My thoughts are always like the thistledown—a thought of Harry Lynch has darted across my mind. It is perfectly disgraceful that I have not sent him *The Lake*. Of course you know that he knows the lake as well as I do, every island, every shore—I must send him the book tomorrow. I have written page after page without speaking of Mrs

[1] This must refer to the story called "The Lovers of Orelay" in *Memoirs of my Dead Life* (1906). The name Orelay was coined for G.M. by John Eglinton, who is certain that the actual town was Avignon. It is tempting to protract the interpretation of this reference, and to equate the Doris of the story with Maud, but further evidence is lacking.

[2] G.M.'s spelling was so erratic that it is difficult to distinguish a pun from an error.

Cotton. Is she out of danger? Her recovery shows how little doctors know of life and death, how inscrutable are the two great mysteries. When you see her will you tell her how much I rejoice in her recovery. I should like to write to her myself and I would if I knew her out of danger.

As ever George Moore

30 March [*1906*]   *4 Upper Ely Place*
                                                        Dublin

Do not trouble about the fur-lined overcoat. You gave me a comb twelve years ago and I have the pieces still. I'd much sooner have a letter from you than all the fur in Canada. I suppose what you say is true about the dream. For days before I was uneasy and expectant, and it is pretty to think if it be not true (though I see no reason why it shouldn't be true) that some sort of electrical sympathy should exist between people who have known each other a long while and thought about each other. I cannot imagine a greater act of madness than to pay £280 for a bronze of Wyndham's bust.[1] You will hate it when it has been in your house a month. Rodin told me that whosoever had his bust done by him could have bronzes of it at 1000 francs—£40. The Wyndham bust is one of Rodin's worst. If you must have something else, get the Victor Hugo or the [Jean-]Paul Laurens; those are among his good things. Better still get your bust done, he told me he would do a bust of you for £500, and then I shall be able to have a bronze for 60, 80 or 100. No matter. I beseech you not to buy the Wyndham. When will you write to Orpen? Do sit to him for a drawing—I must have a drawing of you. The photograph you gave

[1] Rodin made a bust of the statesman and writer George Wyndham (1863–1913) in the summer of 1904.

me is a great pleasure to me, it hangs in my bedroom and I see it every morning. But if I had an Orpen drawing I should see you fifty times a day. About Howard. I wonder if there is anything in this Druce case.[1] Howard's aunt told me he had 170 thousand a year, and he has neither wife nor children, nor does he entertain. I wouldn't write to anybody else but you on this matter, but I can't help discussing it with you. However if Howard falls the Duke of Portland falls too, and his fall will be the greater, for he becomes Mr Bentinck. You know you can tell me what you like, so do write me the news if you should happen to hear any in connection with the case. Has the syndicate begun proceedings? When does the case come on for hearing? I wonder if you would care to see the proofs of my new book, really care. I should not like you to show them. *The Lake* was the biggest success I have had, so far as the newspapers are concerned. I thought at first it had fallen quite flat.

As ever George Moore

[1] Lord Howard de Walden had inherited some part of the Portland estates, and in 1907 it was estimated that the joint fortunes of the two families amounted to £16,000,000. Since 1896 various descendants of a Baker Street shopkeeper named T. C. Druce (*d.* 1864) had been endeavouring to prove that Druce had never existed, but had been an alias of the fifth Duke of Portland (*d.* 1879), whose known eccentricities were extravagantly improbable. If they could prove their case, some part of the great fortune must be theirs, and perhaps the dukedom as well. For eleven years these extraordinary proceedings dragged on through police courts, the Lord Mayor's Court, the House of Lords, the Consistory Court in St Paul's, and the Old Bailey. The final action (for perjury) took place in 1907, and the claims were finally exploded when Druce's coffin was opened and found to contain his body. See *The Druce-Portland Case* by Theodore Besterman (1935).

3 November [Postmark 1906]   4 Upper Ely Place
                                        Dublin

I suppose you are in New York for the winter . . . the change will amuse you and it will amuse Nancy. Do speak to her sometimes of me, for I don't want her to forget me. As I have written before, I am sentimental as an old ballad . . . but you don't like that. As for you, I think of you as I have always done, as a joy that knows no diminishing—you are the magic apple which however much one eats of it never grows less. I have something to propose to you but am without hope that you will comply; it is that you land at Cork and come on here to see me and your pictures. You have Nancy with you, so you can come. It would give me such pleasure to see you here that it is a pity you can't come, for my instinct tells me that you won't come for one reason or another. You want to hear perhaps about my writings. . . the Americans will not publish the *Memoirs* without omissions and I have consented to the omissions on condition that I write a preface; and I have written one on morality in life and literature. *Cause and Cure* would be a good title. Appleton is publishing the book. You will be able to get a copy much sooner than I shall. The book will be out when you get this letter. Why not ask for it . . . there are things in it that will amuse you and interest you, things that do not appear in the English edition.[1]

As ever, dear Maud, George Moore

[1] The text of the first American edition (1906) of *Memoirs of my Dead Life* differed slightly from that of the first English edition. G.M.'s preface, entitled *Apologia Pro Scriptis Meis*, was never reprinted, though in 1922 he used the same title for his introduction to the first volume of the Carra Edition of his works (see note, p. 122).

6 April 1907   *4 Upper Ely Place*
                                                              Dublin

One is not always fortunate, and the last time I saw you
was an unlucky day. But you shouldn't allow an unlucky
day to prejudice you, there are unlucky days in every life,
and we have known each other so long that your memory
can easily find a happier occasion to rest upon. You said
that I was not a true friend of yours—you could not have
meant what you said, you could not have been so de-
ceived: you know that I prize nothing on earth as much
as you and that I shall die thinking of you. Do write me a
line, for I am really unhappy.

                         Yours always George Moore

13 August [1907][1]   *4 Upper Ely Place*
                                                              Dublin

It was delightful to get your happy letter. Of course
you enjoyed your season, we all enjoy what we do well
and your life is a work of art. I work with ink and paper,
the sculptor takes a block of marble, the painter pigments
and canvas, the actor, it is true, takes himself but he has
to get an author to write for him and a scene-painter to
paint for him; he requires rouge and limelights—you require none of these things and the result is more astonish-
ing. I wonder if you ever see yourself—I fancy not, you
are very little spectator—I mean *que vous êtes si peu*

[1] The original of this letter is among the papers of the late Lord
Howard de Walden. G.M. had recently written to him: "I want you
to find out from Lady Cunard why she doesn't write to me. There
is no use writing to ask her, but if you should see her she might
tell you. You know how long I have known her and what an in-
timate friend she is. She makes me feel I'm alive. Several letters have
remained unanswered and several telegrams. Do this I beg of you."
Presumably Lord Howard complied, Lady Cunard wrote G.M. a
"happy letter" and sent G.M.'s answer to Lord Howard as proof.

spectateur. Perhaps you would not be so wonderful if you were self-conscious . . . To-night I am feeling depressed and life seems a weariness. I have come in from a little walk, but it has not freshened my spirits. These fits of depression come after long periods of work. You will say, why not cease to work and go somewhere for a change? This cannot be, work taken up must be finished, added to this it would be unwise to spend money now; Consols are down to 80 and this slump in the money market is making the sale of land in Ireland an impossibility.[1] The work I am engaged on will not bring me any money. Things do not look very rosy. We all have our troubles and mine are very slight compared with Lord Grimthorpe's. He has managed to pull through, and to-day I see his name mentioned in the newspapers as the probable successor to Lord Sefton, who is retiring from the ministry.[2] Your kindness in asking me to Holt in October touched me; it isn't probable that I shall be able to come, but thank you all the same. You have always been the best and truest friend. There is no one like you, Maud—no one as fascinating, no one as clever, no one as good; and every year it seems to me that I see you in a more beautiful light. But why are you going to Marienbad? People go there to be cured, but of what? I can't make out, men and women. I'll write to you again. But of what shall I write—what would you like to hear?

As ever George Moore

I wrote to Howard the other day but have not had an answer. I am afraid that like another he is not always happy.

[1] On 12 August 1907 Consols fell below 81.

[2] Neither the second Lord Grimthorpe (see note p. 28) nor the sixth Earl of Sefton (1871-1930) was ever a minister, but Lord Sefton did relinquish his position as Master of the Horse in 1907.

I think one should answer letters at once, while one is *sous le coup de l'émotion* produced by the letter. But your letter arrived just as I was leaving Seaford House and for the last couple of days I have been engaged on what I suppose I must call literary work. Your letter was one of the most interesting you have written me for a long time; it might have been much more interesting if it had been longer and more explicit. However it was good enough to suggest an idea to me—suppose we begin a correspondence with a view to some possible publication later on. For this correspondence to be interesting it must be sincere and it must be complete; you must confess your frailties and I will answer that my love is above all transgressions on your part. It will be quite easy to avoid including anything that might reveal our identities—you are a lady of high degree and I am a writer. The present and the past are in the letters what they were in reality—this sentence is not quite English. The present is—I cannot see the present in the past tense. The correspondence will be affectionate, amorous and literary; each letter should be at least as long as a leading article in *The Times* and to write such letters two things are required—courage and application. If you care to undertake it I will tell you where it should begin.

Howard's play is going on very well. He showed me just before I left the last scene of his Welsh play—the description of the destruction of the ancient Britons.[1] It seemed to me quite splendid, as good as anyone might wish to write. To you belongs the discovery of Howard's

[1] *Dylan, Son of the Wave*, a dramatic poem, written in 1904. In 1914 it formed the libretto for an opera by Josef Holbrooke. It was published in 1918, and again in a limited edition in 1922 as part of a trilogy called *The Cauldron of Annwn*.

Mr George Moore, Preacher to Lord Howard de
Walden, by Max Beerbohm, 1907

literary genius. And I pooh-poohed you but you didn't change your opinion. Bravo.

But how am I to live many months without seeing you? Candidly I don't know. I have seen so much of you lately that I am demoralised—in the sense that I am no longer independent. My eyes turn to Leicestershire as the sunflower turns to the sun. Could you come to Ireland in the autumn? Lady Burroughs I am sure would be delighted to see you—you know who I mean, Howard's aunt. I think Howard and I are sincere friends, and I owe him to you. Dear friend, when I think of the joy you have been to me, the benedictive hopes and aspirations you have inspired, I am overcome; I cannot understand how such a thing could have come across my life's way, such a spirit, such a fountain of delight. The hours I spend with you I look upon as a sort of perfumed garden, a dim twilight and a fountain singing to it. But months will have to pass without my seeing you. Shall I be able to endure this long exile? I met a man in the train I knew, one of the partners in the firm of Agnew, and he complained I had not been writing. I answered, I have been living. You and you *alone* make me feel that I am alive.

As ever George Moore

30 March [*1908*]   4 *Upper Ely Place*
Dublin

Alas I am here till August writing, and am feeling very disappointed, for a visit to Holt is what I like best. Tomorrow or after I shall write to Nancy upbraiding her for not writing from New York as she promised. I knew you would not, but you are never as bad as you seem, for you don't forget and you have invited me to Holt. It seems strange that your active pursuit of the ideal man should have resulted in your discovery of the ideal woman.

I discovered my ideal thirteen years ago, or what serves me as an ideal, and the eternal hunt ended so far as I was concerned. The loss of your sables is very great. Is there no hope of recovering them? Thousands of dollars! Good heavens! Howard's play is going to be acted on the 13th or the 15th of May and I think it will astonish people, but don't talk about it—he doesn't wish it talked about and he'll be annoyed if you do.[1] I spent some time with him before I went to France and after I returned from France. In France I had the pleasure and the privilege of hearing a masterpiece—the first lyrical work of first-rate importance which France has produced—*Ariane et Barbe-Bleue*.[2] You have money and leisure and you should start off at once to see it. Life is made up of things which when we are close to them seem very small but which grow larger as the distance widens between us. I am expressing myself badly, as I always do when I am writing in a hurry, but you will understand. Go to Paris to see *Ariane et Barbe-Bleue* and you will bring back an imperishable souvenir. You know that I have always been able to distinguish between a wash-tub and a vase, and *Ariane et Barbe-Bleue* is a vase beyond question.[3] Kiss Nancy for me and tell her I look forward to hearing from her and going for a walk with her.

Ever yours George Moore

[1] *Lanval*, an Arthurian drama in four acts by T. E. Ellis (Lord Howard de Walden), was produced at the Playhouse Theatre on 15 May 1908 with music by Poldowski and scenery by Charles Ricketts.

[2] This opera by Paul Dukas, with libretto adapted from Maeterlinck's play, was first produced at the Opéra Comique, Paris, on 10 May 1907.

[3] Cf. *Ave* (1911), p. 61. "And in every art he [the 'boon companion'] must be able to distinguish between wash-tubs and vases; he must know instinctively that Manet is all vase, and that Mr ——'s portraits are all wash-tub."

George Moore in Dublin, 23 January, 1908; a photograph
by Alvin Langdon Coburn

9 April 1908   *4 Upper Ely Place*
                                          Dublin

There is a gentleman who lives near Dublin in a large
and commodious house furnished with heavy and com-
fortable Victorian furniture; he is attended by numerous
servants, breakfasts well, lunches upon toast and chicken
and claret, and his dinner I believe is as excellent and as
copious as his lunch. He farms a little and plays golf too.
So far you know many such men; the only difference
between the man I am speaking of and those who live
about your doors is that my man has been painting beautiful pictures all his life without ambition, from sheer love
of painting. He does not give away his pictures but he
sells them very cheaply, and if you want a "work" I can
buy you one for about £30, a landscape, pastures which
one guesses to be not very far from the sea with moving
herds of cattle; or a large estuary flowing through a silent
country where no one speaks and a lugsail catches the wind.
Of course if you don't want a picture there is no use buying
one, but if you do want a picture for your house I can send
you some sketches at five pounds apiece or real works at
thirty or forty pounds. I'd recommend you to take a
"work"—the "work" is generally in Nathaniel Hone's
case preferable to the sketch.[1] I am still looking for the
dessert service and hope to get it. Howard has some plates
and if you go to Seaford House you can see them. I shall
write to Nancy tomorrow. She, dear thing, will answer
my letter.

                                   As ever George Moore

[1] Nathaniel Hone, R.H.A. (1831–1917). G.M. had contributed a
prefatory note to the catalogue of an exhibition of Hone's pictures in
Dublin in 1901. See *Four Irish Landscape Painters* by Thomas Bodkin
(1920).

25 April [1908][1]   *4 Upper Ely Place*
                                                        Dublin

I should like to write you a long letter, a letter full of
long parenthetical sentences, commas everywhere and
plenty of dashes, for only in such a style may emotions
be expressed: and when I think of Holt emotions rather
than thoughts rise up, and though they are intense they
are so vague that words will not hold them; only in
music might they be conveyed and I am not a composer,
only an ignorant lover of the emotional ballads which
you will soon be able to play very well. How my thoughts
drift to that oak gallery, and it was kind of you to give
me a room facing the schoolroom. I liked my visits to
Nancy's schoolroom and my walks with her in the wood
where the windflowers grow, and the wellheads whither
the eighteenth century came to drink the water. I would
not omit a mention of our delightful drive to Leicester;
it is always a pleasure to go to a picture gallery with you—
you are the only woman one can go with, for you never
say anything stupid about pictures, or indeed about any
art. The one woman in Society who can talk about art
without making a fool of herself is Maud Cunard . . . I
am vexed because I cannot find some phrases which
would tell you how gay and smiling life seems when one's
friends seem to love one; happiness has always been my
quest, I have always flown to that lure—to the lure of
friendship, never having been able to disassociate happiness from friendship. I am as gregarious as yourself or
very nearly. But for me there is but one bird in the flock.
True it is that we all seek happiness, and if my case is in
any way peculiar it is because I appreciate the beauty of
the sunny hour when one forgets oneself, and you and
Nancy make me forget everything else. So my visit to

[1] G.M. signed the Nevill Holt visitors book on 21 April 1908.

58

Holt was a complete success from my point of view; the only speck upon my happiness is that perhaps you did not enjoy me as much as I enjoyed you. You lack one thing —memory; and it is memory that gives life its fragrance. But this letter is concerned too much with the emotions, so I will escape out of them into finger-glasses. I find that Waterford glass finger-glasses will cost as much as a pound apiece. Would you care to pay as much? You forwarded a letter from Lord Howard; he wrote asking me to come to Seaford House and setting my mind at rest regarding the alterations—he is only condensing the dialogue; you must have misunderstood him. Do go to see his play and "dictate" a letter. If you like I'll recommend an excellent shorthand writer.

Remember me to Sir Bache and to Miss Scarth[1] and give Nancy my love.

As ever George Moore

25 May [*1908*]   *4 Upper Ely Place*
                                                      Dublin

Dear vision, dear and divine, come down to me through many generations from the time when there were gods upon the earth, but losing nothing in this long transmigration of the original loveliness, I write to thank thee for thy last kindnesses to me a mortal but a worshipper of the essential. These lines will seem exaggerated to thee, for among ages which accept nothing as divine the goddess forgets her divinity without however losing any particle of it. But of such heavy substance is our human life made that it may rise above the earth only a little way; it must fall back soon from thou to you under penalty of seeming ridiculous, so turning from the immortal to the mortal I beg to say that tomorrow I hope to send you twenty-four Wedgwood green dessert plates, vine-leaf

[1] Nancy Cunard's governess.

59

pattern; the dishes which are the most beautiful part of the service are unprocurable for the moment: I hope to obtain one which will serve as a pattern, and some of the London dealers will be able to get five more for you. Your health continues to cause me much uneasiness and it is my belief that a short season in town would suit you better than a long one; were you to go away at the end of June for a rest cure a good deal of firm health might come of it. Of course rest is a bore but ill health is the greatest bore of all. If I could only persuade you. About myself there is nothing to say except that I am here among my pictures writing *Sister Teresa*, but you know nearly as much about her as I do myself.[1] My secretary is as satisfactory as ever, and we are working away beginning at 10.30 and ending every day at 5.30. She was interested to hear about Lord Howard, for she knows him well through me and she knows you, and our visit to Meredith impressed her very much, but like ourselves she doesn't care much for his novels. His poetry is the better part of him; when one is a poet one is always a poet and all that is good in his novels is the poetry they contain . . . The Huntingtons are away now. Poor little woman[2]! She too would like adventure, so you say, and to be watched or looked after is always a bore, especially when the watching is inspired by moral intentions. Dear vision, dear and divine, how shall I tell anew the one thing which seems to me worth telling, that all I am capable of

[1] The edition of *Sister Teresa* which appeared in 1909 was a completely rewritten version of the original book of 1901.

[2] Helen Manchester Gates (?1864-1950) of Wisconsin married (1) a Mr Criss; (2) in 1895 Archer M. Huntington (born 1870), a millionaire who treated her with great generosity; (3) in 1918 Harley Granville Barker (1877-1946), the actor, producer and dramatist. As Helen Huntington she published some novels and volumes of verse. Later she collaborated with Granville Barker in the translation of Spanish plays into English.

conceiving of immortality I see in thee. Other men it
is said have seen angels but I have seen thee and thou art
enough. A light, a beauty, a grace—how often I have used
these words. Divine vision, if not divine to all men
divine at least to me, *au revoir*.

George Moore

8 July [*1908*]   *4 Upper Ely Place*
Dublin

I did not write before because I could make no arrangements till I had heard from Seaford House—I had forgotten the date of our start. Mr Bellingham wrote yesterday saying Lord Howard hoped to leave on the 10th of
August—he mentioned that you, Sir Bache and Nancy
had been at Audley End.[1] Your proposal that I should
spend a fortnight at Holt is delightful, for to me short
visits are not nearly as agreeable as long ones, and if you
will read and play to me in the evening I shall believe
myself in heaven. A fortnight's visit is the thing, but how
is it to be managed? I am hammering away here at *Sister
Teresa* and would like to get on with it. You will not be
at Holt till August and I shall have to be at Seaford House
at latest on the ninth, so it seems impossible to get in a
fortnight at the beginning of August. We shall not be
back from Germany before September—that's certain.
My visit to Holt is my great pleasure and I am not going
to miss going there *coûte que coûte*, so will you let me know
when you can have me. I owe Nancy a letter; the dear
thing sent me a few wildflowers but it was too early in
the year, the season is a late one; I must ask her if there are
any wild forget-me-nots in the hedges at this season.

As ever George Moore

Do you remember reading *The Frogs*?

[1] Lord Braybrooke's Jacobean house in Essex, which Lord Howard
de Walden had rented from his kinsman.

In our 'elegant' modern idiom the American lady 'turned up' and during the interval between the acts she asked me to go to church with her today and with my usual gallantry I consented, but to my horror I discovered her church to be a papist edifice from which I retreated as a good Irish protestant would, and in your idiom 'made tracks' for my own church. After service, feeling myself to be dressed appropriately (I wore my grey suit, frock coat and top hat), I went to the lady's lodging and explained to her that a radical difference in our religious opinions rendered our happiness impossible. She feebly conceded one or two sacraments, but unappeased I bade her goodbye, and the breakfast of which we were to partake has been indefinitely postponed. True it is the lady's bosom is voluminous, and a large bosom is my detestation (I arrive by the aesthetic route), but though the physical influenced me, it would seem the religious motive was the determining one, or should I say preceded the physical. There are always two motives; in this case there were three, and perhaps a thought of you decided me not to go to Paris with the lady. I must believe in the goddess. Without belief the act of love is without taste or significance for me, and only in one woman do I perceive the goddess; only from her do I draw the inspiration which the *Walküre* afforded me yesterday—the most extraordinary performance ever given! I swear it. The three voices—bass, tenor and soprano—suited each other, each enhanced the other.[1] Never did I hear so beautiful a brown or so beautiful a red or so beautiful a blue, and never did I appreciate the woman which Wagner

[1] The three singers were Allen Hinckley (Hunding, bass), Alfred von Barry (Siegmund, tenor), and either Katherine Fleischer-Edel or Martha Leffler-Burkard, who alternated in the role of Sieglinde, soprano.

was dreaming when he wrote the scene when Sieglinde after giving Hunding the sleep potion comes down to Siegmund, who lies by the fire, and tells him the misfortunes that await him—the misfortunes inherent in their lives. Rembrandt in some portraits of women has managed to throw the vague diffused life of woman upon the canvas. (Man's life is more definite, it seems to me, than woman's; woman is all instinct.) And suddenly to enforce the idea, this idea, the melancholy Valhalla motive is heard and Sieglinde appears in all the sorrow of her sex; and I said to myself with some bitterness: "Wagner has done more in five minutes than I have done in 365 pages". Only for one moment did my attention wander—when it occurred to me that I could write a beautiful article about the performance. The singing was so perfect that when Fricka went wrong (once she went wrong) one felt that one had returned to earth where things are not always flawless. The long soliloquy is too intolerably wrong, for it is without musical interest; Wagner ought to have lived five years longer, for I have such respect for his genius that I feel sure he would have spent these years in contracting his too lengthy tails;[1] and the length of this scene and the length of the Walküre scene and the argument with Brünhilde leave one too tired to enjoy the beautiful song which Wotan sings before laying his daughter on the rock where she is to sleep till the pure hero kisses her. Today we shall hear *Siegfried*, and the singer is the finest I have yet seen. The singer is a mad doctor; he suddenly discovered that he had the finest dramatic tenor [voice] in Germany, and he is also a fine dramatic actor.[2] My dear Maud, it is wonderful, and Bayreuth is the most enchanting place in the world, or would be if you were here to appreciate the great genius

[1] Perhaps G.M. meant to write "tales".

[2] The part of Siegfried (tenor) was sung by Alois Burgstaller.

63

who created it all. Here all is Wagner; all the streets lead to the theatre, and about the wooded hill are beautiful undulating hills, very Roman (*dans le goût de Poussin*), and after the second act the blue dusk consecrates the landscape and it becomes a single impression of severe, noble beauty. My pen runs over the paper, I hardly know what I am writing—there is no time for composition. Howard is learning German downstairs with the House-wife, who I think enjoys teaching him. Carriages go by every moment. How I wish you were here, *vous qui êtes tellement musicienne*. You would hear more than I hear.

Au revoir George Moore

Tuesday [Postmark 18 August 1908]   *Bayreuth*

Yesterevening on the hill top amid the pine woods through which one caught glimpses of the blue-grey valley rising up into hills till a long undulating crest like a musical phrase showed against the sky, I again approached the burning question of should we or should we not, and firmly but with moderation compelled the lady to understand that an Irish protestant could not enter a papist's bed, and that if overpowered by a sudden access of sense he were to yield there was little doubt that during a night of intolerable mental anguish his razor would be seized and mutilation would follow. She listened as women listen to men, pathetically. A kind woman at heart, who asked Howard and me to dinner notwith-standing the disappointment. I was for escaping from the dinner, but Howard insisted that after beguiling the lady so far I must treat her with consideration, and he called my attention to her patient face during *The Dusk of the Gods*. A point I should like to make is that if Wagner had not been interrupted in the composition of *Siegfried* his gigantic artwork would have failed. Whether the interruption came from without or from within—from some prompting of his subconscious self—we do not know; however this may be, it seems certain that he had pursued the method to the tedious end in *Siegfried*. I allude to his practice of uttering the motive whenever the person or thing with which the motive was associated is mentioned; this practice seems to me to become a trick in the first and second acts, and the result a sort of patchwork quilt—I can compare the first and second acts to nothing else. The folklore so charming in *The Rhinegold* begins to get tedious in *Siegfried*, so it was well that an interruption came, an interruption of many years during which his style enlarged. The third act compensates us for the first two acts—these acts are beautiful if we hear the opera by itself, but coming after the *Walküre* and preceding *la beauté fulgurante* of *The Dusk of the Gods* they seem small and often drift into tediousness. *The Dusk of the Gods*, notwithstanding its length, passed quickly without a moment of *ennui*. The scene with the horns especially delighted me—the three voices singing the wild eloquent music amid the rocks, "the Question to Fate" not intruded too frequently, struck me as the highest scarp or cliff that human genius has reached. Wagner's music in *The Dusk of the Gods* is extraordinarily eloquent; eloquence is generally a term of reproach, but Wagner's eloquence is so necessary for the sustenance of the work that one accepts it with thanks and admiration. To compare a small thing with a great thing seems to me permissible, everything is permissible when the intention is to explain one's meaning; besides, this letter is addressed to one who seizes every subtle meaning and never thinks it worth while to indulge in superficial perversions. You are such a one; therefore I have no hesitation in speaking of De Quincey's prose, the faults of which anyone can see, but to which it seems to me impossible to deny an overflowing eloquence of expression, rising up naturally as an ardent spring and carrying the reader away on its splendid current. This same extraordinary and natural eloquence which never falters I hear in *The Dusk of the Gods*, enforced, of course, by other qualities far higher, by a dramatic nobility of intention never possessed by man before. But notwithstanding his gift of eloquence and notwithstanding the diversity of *The Ring*, *il est toujours dans son sujet*. Added to the charm of the work there came the charm of the interpretation: ten years ago I heard Gulbranson, and yesterday her voice was stronger and purer and her management of her voice more perfect. She is a plain woman but her smile transforms her—her smile is not a mere mechanical dribble about the lips—an actress's smile is often no more—her smile flows up from within, suffusing the face with its light. Richter seemed to me to be in a bad temper—he took the music at an incredible pace, on one occasion certainly hurrying Gulbranson, not allowing her time to get the whole of her voice. There are some high notes in the final scene, which brings gods and heroes to an end, and these she took as easily as she would notes in the middle of her voice. After these terrific scenes we saw her in the restaurant; she came down the long room smiling amid salvos of applause—delighted in the praise she was receiving, and there is nothing more charming than to see the recipient of praise accepting praise gracefully. If I knew German I should have gone to her and told her of the great pleasure her singing had given me. She sat amid her friends talking and eating, apparently not in the least tired and enjoying herself immensely. Life as it came to her seems to have come as a perfect gift.

Au revoir, dear Maud. I am looking forward to seeing you. May I stay a day or two at Holt on my way back to Ireland? We return to England on Friday. Do write to

Seaford House. I'd like to find a letter from you awaiting my arrival. Perhaps I shall try to relieve the barrenness of Ireland in *Hail and Farewell* with the description of a visit to Bayreuth, so will you keep these letters or have them copied. Perhaps they might help me.[1]

Au revoir again.

As ever George Moore

3 October [1908]   *4 Upper Ely Place*
                                                        Dublin

My dear,

I am better and I have read Mrs Huntington's book and like the dear little story.[2] I shall write to her on Monday and will send you a copy of my letter—there is no use writing the same things twice over. So Venice is divine—divine are the eyes that saw Venice. My comedy is finished and it is the dearest *little* comedy in the world;[3] of that I am quite sure, but its manifest beauty will bring it distinction, for nowadays a play must be like a poster, green figures on a purple background with a red pig in the corner, something you can see half a mile off. I saw *Jack Straw* last Tuesday and was amused notwithstanding its garishness.[4] Florence St John played the old woman, and I never saw a part better played. Is Mrs Huntington with you or shall I send my letter to America? She

[1] The only use G.M. made of this material in *Hail and Farewell* was a brief reference to Gulbranson in the restaurant after the opera, *Ave* (1911), pp. 220–21.

[2] *The Sovereign Good*, by Helen Huntington (1908). The heroine is called Fidelia (see notes, pp. 60 and 68).

[3] *Elizabeth Cooper*. See note p. 33.

[4] *Jack Straw*, by W. Somerset Maugham, was first produced at the Vaudeville Theatre on 26 March 1908, with Charles Hawtrey in the title-role. The part of Mrs Parker-Jennings, created by Lottie Venne, was after some months taken over by Florence St John.

publishes in America. Will you write, for it would be a
pity if the letter were so long delayed.

As ever George Moore

Please write or send me a wire.

Saturday [31 October 1908]   *4 Upper Ely Place*
                                                          Dublin

My dear,

I feel so dreadfully guilty for having left you without
a letter so long that I write this on Saturday in the hopes
that several postage stamps will bring it to you tomorrow
morning. My excuses are always the same, literature is
a vile excuse, but since hearing from you I have been
engaged on the last chapter of *Sister Teresa*—the meeting
between Owen Asher and Evelyn when she retreats from
the convent, nearly a short book in itself. It was kind of
you to write to me about my letter to Mrs H. She wrote
me a very charming artless little letter quite in her own
manner in the style of the book, thanking me. It was
rather amusing her determination that poor Fidelia[1] who
isn't virtuous at all should be so narrow, but we are all
anxious that somebody else should be virtuous. I remember a little boy who was very naughty and when his
parents told him he was so naughty that he must pray to
be good he was naughty enough to say that he would not
be good and would not pray to be good. The nurse was
appalled at this infantile wickedness and was hardly satisfied when the little boy agreed to kneel down and pray
that his little brother should be good. Tomorrow night
I am looking forward to seeing Esposito;[2] he is going to
give a recital and he has asked me to come to hear his

[1] See note, p. 67.
[2] Michele Esposito (1855–1929), Italian pianist and composer, was
Professor of Pianoforte at the Royal Irish Academy of Music in
Dublin from 1882 to 1928.

programme; it will be so much nicer to hear the music in his own house. He is playing Chopin's third ballade. But I'm afraid you'll think I am flattering you when I tell you that I think you play it better. Of course Esposito is a wonderful pianist, but his playing is a little cold and he doesn't bring out the rich romanticism of Chopin's nature which you understand so extraordinarily well. I beg of you not to think I am flattering you. I am just telling you my feeling. True that I heard him play the ballade on a bad piano, perhaps he'll play it better than you do tomorrow night on his new piano, but quite sincerely I don't think he will. I'll write on Monday for certain and tell you.

Ever yours George Moore

4 November [*1908*]   *4 Upper Ely Place*
Dublin

I went to Esposito's on Sunday night and he played to me the pianoforte recital which he gave on Monday at the Royal Dublin Society. He played the Appassionata Sonata as well as it was ever played, and it is the finest sonata ever written. Beethoven must have had an orchestra in his head as he wrote—one hears the clarionets, oboes, etc., all the time. Then my dear friend played two ballades of his own or three, I've forgotten. They are very well written but he doesn't seem to me to be able to follow a melody. Beethoven presents the melody in all its phases—you know the sonata. His own ballades were followed by a berceuse by Chopin which he played very delicately—I don't know if you play it always the same, bass with variations of the melody in the treble. And then he played the third ballade in a way which is my detestation. I think you will be able to form an exact idea of his playing of this romantic piece when I tell you that as played by him it reminded me of a drawing in lead pencil of a picture by Rubens or Watteau or Monticelli; a picture full of romantic colour and romantic chiaroscuro and elusive distances interpreted by means of a lead pencil. It was very correct no doubt but anything less romantic I cannot imagine. I told him so, and he said somebody has been playing it to you and you have got his or her reading into your head and you'll never like mine. Then he got angry and said I wanted it played with effusion and tears and that if anybody played it like that for him he would turn the player out of the room. Everything is arguable in this world (except papistry) and of course the whole romantic school can be sponged out. Ingres believed that no man could paint like Delacroix if he were not morally infamous. I'm sorry I dragged in Ingres who to me is a great romanticist. When I go to London I shall try to hear some great pianists play the ballade in question, only in that way can I find out which is the true rendering—if there is such a thing as a true rendering: I prefer yours and shall always prefer it, and that is all, my dear friend, I've to tell you today.

Give my love to Nancy and write to me soon.

As ever George Moore

31 March 1909   *4 Upper Ely Place*
                                                        Dublin

In the beginning of last year I came over to London for change of air after a bad attack of influenza. So I can sympathise with you. But if you are going to Italy on Saturday you must be much better, and if you are still sick the change of air will put you right at once. There is so much to say that I know not how to write this letter . . . I want to tell you briefly that I have posted a letter to Miss Kauser saying that if she will send me back the comedy

70

I'll finish it.[1] That's what it wants, finishing. I could not allow it to be played in its present form. The subject is such a pretty one that I must *lui donner une toilette parfaite*. In Paris at the beginning of this year I spent a most enjoyable month with my old friends and a few new ones. I picked up the Daudet thread again and find the family most interesting. But if I begin to tell you about my conversations with Lemaître[2] and a quantity of other things which would amuse you, I shall miss the post and my walk which I require badly for I've been writing all day. I have just completed a long long preface for *Sister Teresa*. The length of the preface and its complications you will be able to guess when I tell you that Matthew Arnold and Sainte-Beuve are in it.[3] Sainte-Beuve regards the rewriting of my book as Porbus and Poussin regard the repainting of Frenhofer's picture in Balzac's *Chef-d'Œuvre Inconnu*.[4] Give Nancy my love and tell her I hope she will enjoy Italy and will have a great deal to tell me when she comes back; and remember me to Sir Bache. This is no letter at all. I'll write again.

As ever George Moore

3 June [?*1909*]   *4 Upper Ely Place*
Dublin

Just a line to thank you for writing to me. When I read that your life had been despaired of for two days I thought

[1] Alice Kauser was a leading New York play-agent.

[2] François Elie Jules Lemaître (1853–1914), French critic and dramatist.

[3] On 11 April 1909 G.M. wrote to Edmund Gosse: "I spent a month writing a dialogue between Matthew Arnold and Sainte-Beuve but it didn't work out." Another preface was written instead.

[4] It had been painted and repainted so much that nothing recognisable was left. "*Je ne vois là* [*dit Poussin*] *que des couleurs confusément amassées et contenues par une multitude de lignes bizarres qui forment une muraille de peinture.*"

of myself, and what my loneliness would have been if what seemed so impossible had happened, for I cannot believe that you will ever die . . . You were saved to us and that is enough for the present. My intentions are to remain here till August writing. You asked me to come to Holt in August. Would you prefer me to come at the beginning or at the end of the month and for how long? If your invitation is for the end I think I shall go to Bayreuth again, but far beyond and above Wagner is my desire to see you. So will you let me know the time of my visit?

Always the same George Moore

3 July [*1909*]   *4 Upper Ely Place*
Dublin

I had hoped to hear from you this morning or from Nancy—she might just as well write to me as do lessons. I sent you *Sister Teresa* but I don't want you to write to me about it—you are not well enough and there is nothing to write but if you would write about yourself or dictate a letter. This morning I read in the *Irish Times* that Lady Randolph is going to produce a comedy at Hicks' Theatre entitled *In Borrowed Plumes*.[1] This title smacks strangely of *The Peacock's Feathers*[2] and it is very possible that Jenny may be in borrowed plumes.

As ever George Moore

[1] *His Borrowed Plumes* by Mrs George Cornwallis-West (Lady Randolph Churchill's later name) was produced at the Hicks Theatre on 6 July 1909, and was reviewed, not too favourably, by Max Beerbohm in the *Saturday Review* on 10 July (see his *Around Theatres*, 1953, p. 553).

[2] See note, p. 33.

4 September [1909]   Seaford House
                                          Belgrave Square
My dear Blue Bird,[1]
  Why did you say that I didn't seem sorry to lose you?
Because I don't wear my heart always on my sleeve . . . is
that necessary? And do you not know that no one ever
will appreciate you and admire you as I do—never with
the same truthful fervour, for you come out of the ends
of my life—everything led up to the moment when I
first caught the glint of those beautiful wings; and have
I not followed the light of those wings ever since? And
would not the truthful picture of me be, a man following
with outstretched arms? And shall I not die seeing a blue
bird—when sight of all else is gone your beautiful wings
will float in the dimming twilight; beautiful in the
beginning, more beautiful in the end. Unworthy suggestion that I was not grieved at losing you after a month
of happiness—happiness such as only the blue bird's wings
can give.
  Always, O my blue bird, thy devoted and ecstatic
follower   George Moore

[September 1909]   Hotel Continental
                                                  Paris
My dear Blue Bird,
  You write without thinking. If your friend will call
upon me I shall be delighted to see him, to dine with him
and to invite him to dinner. But I cannot call on him, it is
for him to call upon me. I am older than he and I am a
stranger in Paris.
  The servant calls me at a quarter to nine, I drink a cup

[1] Maeterlinck's play *The Blue Bird* was first published (in English)
in 1909 and performed at the Haymarket Theatre in December. The
blue bird is a symbol of happiness.

of coffee and set to work to write my *conférence*.[1] I have
been working now since I arrived in Paris—I had to, no
one was here, the theatres were closed, and to save myself
from the river, the pistol or the phial I had to write. The
experience has been a curious one—writing a long, long
essay in a foreign language is different from writing a
letter, a dedication or a few verses. One's whole mind has
to go into French and that is what mine has done. I
catch myself thinking in French even when I am not
thinking of *la conférence*—no word of English has passed
my lips for the last three days nor a single thought in
English. If I lived here for a year I should know the language.

The *conférence* is full of good things I think. Blanche[2] will
not be in Paris till the end of October. I saw him in Dieppe.
His address is Rue du Docteur Blanche 19, Passy. I shall
be in London en route for Dublin at the end of the month.
I must go to Ireland on the third or fourth.

As ever, dear blue bird, George Moore

4 December [*1909*]   *4 Upper Ely Place*
Dublin

I am sending you back d'Annunzio's book with many
apologies for having kept it so long. If Howard's point is

[1] "*Balzac et Shakespeare*," a long essay in French, was delivered by
G.M. (after coaching from Mademoiselle Richenberg of the Comédie
Française) before a distinguished audience in the Salle des Agricul-
teurs on 18 February 1910. It was printed in the *Revue Bleue* on 26
February and 10 March 1910, and in *Avowals* (1919). An English
translation appeared in the *Century Magazine* of May 1914.

[2] Jacques-Emile Blanche (1861–1942), the painter and lifelong
friend of G.M. For his reminiscences (and portrait) of G.M., see his
Mes Modèles (1928), *Portraits of a Lifetime* (1937), and *More Portraits of a
Lifetime* (1939). G.M. dedicated *Confessions of a Young Man* (1888)
to him.

that I never helped him with the plays at all, there is no use arguing with him or telling him that he has said the exact opposite in a letter.[1] He is a lunatic and there's an end of it. If on the contrary his point is that I did not help him enough to claim authorship, the matter can be settled, for I never proposed to go into the question with him what contribution carries with it a claim to authorship and what doesn't. It was always understood between us that he was to sign the plays. But I cannot sign a paper saying that I never helped him. To do that and to accept his money would be to put a document into his hands whereby he or his heir could charge me with blackmail. Do you understand? He and his advisers seem to have lost their heads completely over this matter.

As ever George Moore

I'm sending you the *Butterfly* containing an article in French on Mallarmé.[2]

29 January [*1910*]   *4 Upper Ely Place*
                                                Dublin

Mrs Hunter has written and telegraphed many times that she will be in Dublin on the 5th and will return on the 11th. As she is coming over to see me it seems to me that it would be a vile action to leave her stranded here. I need not say a word about the pleasure it would be to me to see you two days sooner than I had expected, and you know that I should like to meet Arthur Balfour. I have met him on a few occasions, twice I think, and he is

[1] G.M. had often discussed Lord Howard de Walden's plays with him, particularly *Lanval*, and now claimed to be joint-author on that account. Eventually Lord Howard sent G.M. a cheque for the entire proceeds of the production of Lanval (which came to exactly 17/6) and the dispute was resolved in laughter.

[2] "*Souvenir sur Mallarmé*" by G.M. (with an English translation by Helene Wood) appeared in a short-lived Philadelphia periodical, the *Butterfly Quarterly*, Number 7, Summer 1909.

interested in literature and art quite as much as in politics and would just as lief talk about them as about the elections.[1] I have no difficulty in realising what I lose and how unlucky it all is. It is more than kind of you to invite me to meet Mr Balfour and if I may say it I think I'd suit the occasion as well as another. It is most unfortunate, that I clearly see . . . But I cannot throw over Mrs Hunter any more than I could go out and pick a pocket. If she is not sure she is coming she had better let me know. Would you mind writing to her.

The last letter I got from Howard was a short note saying that he could not continue the correspondence and telling me that I might take legal proceedings against him if I liked. It would be therefore very unpleasant for me to meet him at present and I think you will see that I cannot go to Seaford House. You know the circumstances as well as I do or very nearly, and I can assure you that I have no faintest idea as to what motives actuated his conduct. It is a complete mystery to me and I can only think that he is given to listening to advice from people who would just as lief see us estranged as friendly. But I dare say this surmise is quite wrong, all surmises are. I don't know what to think about him, but I am quite sure that I cannot go to Seaford House for the present.

As ever George Moore

I enclose a telegram just received from Mrs Hunter.

3 March [*1910*]   *Travellers' Club*
Paris

I propose to return early next week and only to stop in London a day, long enough to see you and to bid you

[1] At the General Election in January 1910 Balfour and the Unionists regained more than a hundred seats which had been lost to the Liberals in the landslide of 1906.

goodbye till August when I hope you will be again able to invite me to Holt. I shall work at *Hail and Farewell* all March, April, May, June and July, five months, and then that long work will be finished . . . I hope. The overture appears in the *English Review* for March. Dujardin goes to Palestine tomorrow. If I could write notes I'd write the motive of the Duke's departure—in *Geneviève de Brabant*.[1] But you don't know the dear little operas of the Second Empire. I wish I could spell. . . . But why did you 'wire'? Because you were *too lazy* to write.

As ever, dearest friend, George Moore

[*?23 July 1910*][2]   *Hill Hall*
                                        Theydon Mount
                                        Epping

The most terrible misfortune that could happen to me would be that you should think, for a single moment, that I failed to appreciate your kindness. I am extremely conscious that I failed to answer you adequately yesterday and must beg you to believe that a certain inherent shyness tied my tongue. I wished to tell you how charming you were and how beautiful—though you wore a hat which does not become you as well as some others I have seen you in. But when you took off the hat and all the golden hair flew out I was thankful to the hat that had hidden it, so delightful was the surprise . . . But I could tell you none of these things, for I have not your genius to make a work of art out of life itself—to redeem life from a good—to make life a thing in itself. I have always

[1] An opera by Offenbach, first produced in two acts in 1859, later revised by the composer and lengthened to five acts. This version was first produced in Paris in February 1885, when G.M. probably saw it.

[2] It is impossible to date this letter with certainty. This was the first day on which G.M. signed the Hill Hall visitors book (see note, p. 23), and it seems reasonable to place the letter as early as possible.

felt that there is a goddess in you, and I never felt this more acutely than now. I hope this letter has not worded itself too stupidly. If it has it cannot be helped. I have to go out with Mrs Williamson[1] and it would be unpardonable to keep her waiting any longer.

Au revoir George Moore

I'll come to see you on Monday about six. It will be *I think* impossible to get up to town in time for lunch. I am dependent.

[*?August 1910*][2]

Nevill Holt
Market Harborough

After you left the room I fell asleep hearing the song of a wonderful fountain and seeing the colour changes through the haze of my dreams. G.M.

Tonks and I are talking of the fountain and its endless song and beauty.

MR GEORGE MOORE'S ESCAPE[3]

Crowd charged by Motor-Car

Mr George Moore, the well-known English author, who is at present in Paris on his return from Munich, where

[1] Mrs Hunter's daughter.

[2] According to the Nevill Holt visitors book, this was the only time Tonks and G.M. were there together, though either of them may have failed to sign the book on other occasions. Henry Tonks (1862-1937) was a surgeon before he turned artist and teacher. He was Slade Professor of Fine Arts in the University of London, 1917-30.

[3] The incident here recorded (from the *Continental Daily Mail* of 6 September 1910) is not mentioned in this correspondence or in Hone's *Life*, but G.M. and Lady Cunard were both involved, and G.M.'s account of the accident is unmistakably his own. A long letter from G.M. to his secretary Miss Gough describing the accident belonged to the late Dr Frank L. Pleadwell of Honolulu.

78

he has been attending the musical festivals, has told a representative of the *Daily Mail* of a remarkable motor-car accident which took place the other day in the Bavarian capital, in which two ladies were killed and the novelist himself very narrowly escaped death, while Lady Cunard and another American lady, Mrs Marshall, were injured.

The accident occurred through a chauffeur leaving a large touring automobile by the side of the road just as the crowd was coming out of the Opera late at night. The chauffeur had told his fellow-servant to look after the car while he went on an errand. The servant, to gain time, apparently attempted to move the automobile, which ran with great speed into the crowd outside the Opera. Mr Moore tells the story in his own characteristic style:

> We had arranged to go to supper with Mr and Mrs Perry Belmont after the Opera. There was a drizzle of rain in the air, and Lady Cunard was walking quickly in front. Fearing to lose her I called to her to come back, and she returned to us—that is to Mrs Marshall and myself. A cry went up— a piercing, animal-like cry, and, turning to see what had happened, I saw an immense motor surge up from the street and on to the crowded pavement. I was struck down instantly. "My last moment has come," I said as I lay. But the motor stopped. "I am saved," I said, "but my legs feel broken." The stopping of the motor seemed like a miracle, and the miracle did not seem less when, on taking off my trousers at the hotel, I found the pattern of the nails of the tyre printed all along the torn cloth. Never was anybody nearer death—of that I am sure. I was under the machine for a few moments, unable to rise, and when I was pulled out and it was found that my legs were not broken and that I could stand on them I staggered off in search of Lady Cunard, attracted by the sight of men carrying women away.
>
> But I did not follow far; in my dazed mind the thought passed that I could not speak German and would get lost,

so I came back to the motor, and came upon Lady Cunard, who had just recovered consciousness. A few feet away some men supported Mrs Marshall. I saw pools of blood and shreds of women's dresses—the blood and finery of the women whom I had seen a moment before aloft, borne away like Sabine women by Romans. One of these poor creatures died a few minutes after. The doctors fear there will be many cripples. Mrs Marshall is in hospital, too. She will recover eventually in some months. Lady Cunard was sorely shaken and bruised, and had to keep to her bed for a couple of days, but she is now well, and bore the long journey from Munich to Paris better than might have been expected.

Is it not extraordinary that robbers should be found among a fashionable crowd? There was a rush for scattered purses and their contents. Lady Cunard got back her gold bag, but £20 was missing from it. Mrs Marshall's purse was returned to her, but £10 had been taken from it and some jewellery.

Mr George Moore, who is at present engaged upon a new work entitled *Hail and Farewell*, was, curiously enough, a victim in another motor-car accident last February, when he came to Paris to lecture upon *Balzac and Shakespeare*. It was only by a miracle that he escaped serious injury.

Monday [Summer 1911]   *121 Ebury Street, S.W.*[1]

I bounced out of bed to read your letter and I should be a great writer indeed if I could get on paper the pleasure it gave me to read that you and Nancy speak of me . . . It was a great privation not to have been able to go to Holt, of feeling, affection, sympathy. You and Nancy are my realities—all the others are shadows. The injustice of the interdiction is very flagrant, but you feel it so very

[1] G.M. moved into what was to be his lasting home in the spring of 1911.

keenly that there is no reason for me to insist. So I will pass on and tell you that I look forward to seeing you in September. I shall be in London till Christmas writing *Salve*, but if I were away I should return at once to meet you. The first volume, *Ave*, has been passed for press and will be printed at once.[1] It is your turn to be interested in it—I am now interested in *Salve*. The first hundred pages (typewritten pages) are all about A.E.—A.E. seen through me; but how feeble is the reflection—you know nothing of his writings. I send you *The Hero in Man*,[2] and the poem that I read last night I transcribe:

"Only in my deep heart I love you, sweetest heart.
   Many another vesture hath the soul; I pray
Call me not forth from this. If from the light I part
Only with clay I cling unto the clay.

And ah! my bright companion, you and I must go
   Our ways, unfolding lonely glories not our own,
Nor from each other gathered, but an inward glow
Breathed by the Lone One on the seeker lone.

If for the heart's own sake we break the heart, we may
   When the last ruby drop dissolves in diamond light
Meet in a deeper vesture in another day.
   Until that dawn, dear heart, good-night, good-night."

          Yours as ever, dear heart, George Moore

[*1 or 2*] *September* [*1911*]   *121 Ebury Street*
My dear friend,
   I have just heard that you will not be in London before the 15th of September—I counted on seeing you on the

[1] It was published on 19 October 1911.
[2] A prose pamphlet by A. E. (George Russell, 1867–1935), published (undated) in 1909. The poem that follows is called "A Farewell": it appeared in A.E.'s *The Divine Vision* (1904).

3rd or the 5th. You mentioned these dates in your last dear letter. It is a great disappointment to be put off till the 15th.

Nancy is my informant. I am writing, writing, writing. Miss Gough is going to be married in March and she wants to finish *Salve* with me—*Vale* will be written with a new secretary. She has just got an order to collect sentences from my writings for every day in the year— a calendar—and is very pleased with the job. Our bargain is that I am not to see it till it is published.[1] *Salve* will be finished in March. It will be time for me to take a holiday then—I wonder if I shall see Venice with you.

Yours as ever George Moore

Will my luck stand to me?

[*?8 June 1912*][2]

Mary Hunter is sorry that you do not care to come to

Hill Hall, Theydon Mount, Epping

Dearest Maud,

I am afraid I was not as agreeable as I might have been when you were good enough to call to ask me to come for a drive. But the fault was not mine; the conversation took a wrong turn. I'll try to do better on Tuesday.

Always affectionately yours George Moore

[*Typewritten except for first and last lines*]

21 January 1913   *121 Ebury Street*

My dear Maud,

Your longing to see me was no doubt very acute, but I noticed that you were careful to mitigate your sufferings

[1] *The George Moore Calendar*, selected by Margaret Gough, was published in September 1912.

[2] This date is arbitrary. G.M. signed the Hill Hall visitors book on this day. Lady Cunard first stayed there in July 1913. Thereafter she signed the book on four occasions, but never at the same time as G.M.

by surrounding yourself with a very numerous society. Why you should wish to hear my impressions of the music it is difficult to think, for you know many musicians who will talk to you about it much better than I can; but yielding to my natural inclination to express all my impressions I confess my belief that Holbrooke wrote his music before reading the poem[1] . . . Be this as it may, it would be difficult to find music more inappropriate to the subject than the music he has assigned to it. The first movement of the Moonlight Sonata seems to me nearer to Poe than Holbrooke [is], and I am sure that we should not be very long at the piano before we found something in Chopin much more like Ulalume. Holbrooke seems to me a musical temperament without any faintest intelligence to guide it, a ship without a rudder blown hither and thither.

I do not think that Delius was very wise to write about Paris; Paris is a great deal too big and too various for an art motif. From a smaller town he would have gotten a clearer impression. Wagner, who was always well-advised, chose Nuremberg: in old Nuremberg there were not more than three or four aspects, and an artist does not want more than three or four to create life. Delius seems to distribute his colour very well, and he never lacks a graceful idea, and if he does not draw well, like Conder he can do without drawing and do without it very nicely. The talent of both men seems to me to be on the same plane.

I did not remain till the end of the concert because I wished to fly from your world, which is not my world. You continue to imagine that these people interest me, but you are the only one in Society who interests me. I revolve still but my orbit is a larger one than heretofore.

[1] Josef Holbrooke's symphonic poem *Ulalume*, based on the poem by Edgar Allan Poe, was first performed in London in 1904.

I am now far away, almost invisible. I am Neptune, the oldest of the planets, and am visible through a strong telescope.

A letter came this morning from Lady Amherst asking me to come in during the evening, but I am not feeling very well and am going out of town to a quiet inn whence I shall write to you, perhaps. I wonder if you could take the train from Baker Street? Only if you do, don't bring any ambassadors or ambassadresses.

Always affectionately yours George Moore

23 August [*1913*]   *121 Ebury Street*

My dear Maud,

It is kind indeed of you to invite me to Venice, but were I to accept your invitation I should have to abandon *Vale* which is now about three parts finished. I got a letter—a postcard—from Nancy and she tells me that you find Munich rather boring. I never found it anything else, but I like Bayreuth and nothing will keep me from going there next year; and before and after the performances I should like to stray from one German town to another. A long time ago I spent a summer in Germany and the memory still retains a certain flavour. One of your countrywomen, an admirer of my writings, arrived in Paris about a month ago whence she wrote to me begging me to come over to see her naked. She enclosed a photograph and what do you think, I went and found her waiting for me in an hotel sitting-room. "So my Irishman has come," she said rising.[1]   My love to Nancy.

Always affectionately yours George Moore

[1] G. M. referred again to this incident in *Euphorion in Texas*, first printed in the *English Review* for July 1914 and included in all editions of *Memoirs of my Dead Life* from 1915:

Presently another face rose up in my mind: the straight nose and

28 December [1913]   *Chirk Castle*
                                              Denbighshire
My dear Maud,
   I thought that I was invited for Christmas, but my
invitation was for the New Year and Lady Howard has
asked me to stay on.[1] But I shall return not later than
Friday and all the way back I shall look forward to seeing
you. Howard is more charming than ever. We went for
a walk and climbed a hill whence, if it had not been snow-
ing, we might have seen over half a dozen counties, and
now he is reading a novel in Welsh while I scribble
letters. I have given him your message and he says "that
will be all right". He is a great dear . . . like Jesus Christ—
I mean very much in the same way—an affectionate
nature like myself. I am afraid I am writing nonsense but
it can't be helped, the words are down and I can't begin
the letter again. The numerous servitude have brought in
the tea and Lady Howard will appear presently.
                   Always affectionately yours George Moore

[January 1914]   *121 Ebury Street*
My dear Maud,
   I thought you were coming to dine with me. You
didn't because you feared that you mightn't be amused all
_____
   clear eyes of an American poetess who did not fear that I might be
   disillusioned, for after a long correspondence she sent me some
   snapshots that a girl friend had taken of her while bathing in some
   brook in the Andes; and as these suggested a model that the sculptor
   of the *Venus de Milo* would have implored a sitting from, her letter
   inviting me to come to see her in Paris some two years later was
   welcomed. Here was the chance of seeing in the flesh one of those
   ladies who admired my writings, and I went to Paris, and we met—
   a single meeting with these last words, "And now I cease to be a
   naked woman for you"—one immemorial afternoon in Paris, and
   since then no letter or poem. Nothing.
   [1] Lord Howard de Walden had married Margherita van Raalte
   in 1912. This letter is dated from their visitors book.

the while, and of course life is intolerable if it be not always at concert pitch. I am going away to Syria[1] next month to see a monastery among other things, and perhaps to come back.

Ever yours George Moore

16 *February 1914*   121 *Ebury Street*

My dear Maud,

I'm off to the land of camels and concubines and have ordered 50 of one and 300 of the other. I'll write your name in *Vale* when I return. Give Nancy a kiss for me.

Always yours George Moore

20 *February* [1914]   *P. & O. S. N. Co.*

                                                    S.S. [*Macedonia*]

My dear Maud,

I write to you for I am thinking of you, and I suppose that it has become natural to me to write when I think; and what I am thinking is of your kindness in coming to wish me goodbye. Nancy came a little later and I was touched, and if you would have the exact truth, a little flattered that both of you should have wished to see me. The sea is always kind to me, perhaps because it intends to devour me one day; I crossed from Ireland to England during ten years fifty times at least without seeing a white-crested wave, only languorous ripples; and yesterday I crossed in a dead calm. The journey to Paris differed only in this from my other journeys that I travelled in what is known as *un train de luxe*, but to my mind nothing is less luxurious. One sits boxed up during the day, a panelled partition about a couple of feet from one's face, and at night the sleeping berths on the Bombay

[1] To gather material for *The Brook Kerith*.

86

Express are detestable. A man with two terriers had installed himself in mine and I declined to share the cabin with the dogs. It took a long time to get him out and when he was finally ejected a friend of his was put in with me. Three feet wide and ten feet high may be endurable alone, but with another human being above or below, it makes no difference which, the narrow space becomes a torture "chamber"; and the memory of last night will haunt me for ever. I arrived in Marseilles a wreck and in great fear lest I should have to spend four nights in a similar hole. By application to the Purser I obtained a large cabin—after last night every space seems large—and about noon we steamed alongside of a desert shore—white chalk scarps and hills carven by the wind into many fantastic shapes, seemingly the ruins of a Valhalla builded by gods that have been. And right up to the ghostly shore the bluest and beautifullest of seas[1] rolled gaily as if it remembered gallies of yore. I have forgotten the correct spelling in the plural: galleys or gallies? Both seem equally wrong in my detestable handwriting. During the afternoon a very sweet breeze blew over the boat and the book I was reading fell from my hand. I abandoned myself to the thought that it was about this sea that Man's imagination began; and looked forward to seeing Sicily—the very plain on which Proserpine, while gathering flowers, was raped by Pluto. I remembered that on the opposite shore Aeneas left Dido that he might build Rome, and it seemed to me that I could see Europa carried away on a bull's back. The much admired and the much blamed Helen crossed the sea that I was crossing to Troy and returned to end her life as an excellent wife. The bitter Medea, Jason and the wanderer from Ithaca are all associated with the sea that churns

[1] For a repetition of this phrase, and another brief account of the voyage, see *A Storyteller's Holiday* (1918), chap. ii.

under the window at which I sit writing to you. My love of you has been a long love, and tonight I like to think of it as not unworthy of the Mediterranean, and that is why, perhaps, though I did not know it when I began this letter, I was moved to leave the smoking room to write to you. My letter is finished. It may be that I shall write to you again from Jerusalem, and it may be that I shall write to Nancy instead, for she is more likely than you, dear Maud, to answer my affection with a letter.

Ever yours George Moore

26 February 1914   Grand New Hotel
                                                Jerusalem
My dear Maud,

I have just arrived and my first thought is to seize a pen to write to you. I hope you appreciate the attention. You would like a description of my journey, but the briefest would fill three or four columns of a newspaper —what am I saying?—ten or twelve columns at the very least; and as it is impossible to write as much this evening I must limit myself to saying that I was enchanted with Joppa—with its rags, with its camels, with its donkeys, especially with its rags: sublime are rags on a Beduin's back. Were you to take a piece of cloth and spend ten years soiling it, tearing it, wearing it threadbare and patching it with every bit of cloth and cotton you could find, you would still be far behind the scattered rags that the Beduin carries on his shoulders and that stream about his feet. The hold of our ship was filled with Beduins, Syrians, Jews, children and old men and women —the Mahomedan women veiled. The men would rise suddenly and place a piece of black silk in front of them and fold their hands in prayer. And their prayers absorbed them utterly. All around their fellows emptied out their bags stuffed full of different coloured rags. Some wore long blue chemises, some striped silken vests under a long petticoat of different colours, a dirty yellow predominating. The turbans were of all sorts, the most striking were bound about the head with ropes of camel's hair twisted and dyed. The smell that this crowd of human beings exhaled was a smell of olives and oil slightly rancid. The night was calm but if it had been wild these poor desert wanderers would have been in intolerable agony. Our debarcation is one of my memories —a memory of eyes always avid of colour, form and character. There is no harbour at Joppa and the finest boatmen in the world in their smocks of blue and yellow and their particoloured turbans row about the steamer and simply lift us and carry us down the steps into their great shallow boats. And they carry our trunks, the heaviest, on their backs down the companion ladder, making us feel ashamed of our manhood—a soft effeminate race are we compared to these splendid brown fellows whose muscles are as steel. Their fine guttural language sounds grand in the midst of the blue surges rushing over the reef of rocks—I wish I could write down their strange cries as they pulled at the heavy oars almost joyously, proud of their strength; and I liked their great naked feet propped against the opposite bench so as to get more force into the stroke. The town rises out of the sewage steeply as may be, and when we were carried out of the boat like children we ascended a queer winding laneway stuck between the towering houses—a laneway of drying mud; and it was then I saw my first camel eating some greenstuff in a corner. A string of camels came down the laneway laden with boxes of oranges, their burdens swinging from side to side, and these were followed by donkeys of extraordinary size and beauty—by no means the timid, submissive, alien creature we meet in our

89

islands—the Syrian donkey is a native of the country and he seems to know it; he feels I am sure his citizenship and that he is needed. I should have liked to have spent a few days in Joppa but came on here in the afternoon. The orange gardens surprised me—millions of oranges. And the train passed into hills the most barren and for-bidding—treeless hills whose decaying rocks are scarcely covered with scrub and rough grass. The hills drop into gorges and I began to wonder if I should find the land-scape I require for my story on the other side of Jerusalem —a city whose first aspect repelled me, lines of yellow stone walls built around a high hill . . . My dear Maud, I cannot write any more. You are weary of my letter ere this and I have forgotten to mention the curious shops huddled all the way along the lane that leads up from the sea to the town of Joppa—shops that Nancy would linger in: I dare not venture a guess as to the time it would take to persuade her up the laneway.

Always affectionately yours George Moore

[*late 1915*]   *121 Ebury Street*

My dear Maud,

Alice[1] and I unite in thanking you for your kindness; Alice hopes you will come here soon again so that she may thank you, and I hope that you will come here soon, for all the old reasons, all but one, still hold good. I did [not] go to see you on Saturday not because I didn't want to but because I could not—it is impossible to abandon a difficult chapter before you have gained your end, else a book like *The Brook Kerith* would never be written. I thought that I was going to Mary Hunter's for Christmas but alas she has some shooters coming along.

Ever yours and always affectionately George Moore

[1] G.M.'s housekeeper.

Friday night [*May or June 1916*]   *121 Ebury Street*

I hardly know how to answer your letter, for of course I shall be delighted if you can dine with me, but it would be impossible for me to go with you to hear Martin Harvey—a most unfortunate actor in my opinion. I should pass on my boredom to you, and your evening would be spoilt. I once heard him recite the soliloquy 'To be or not to be' with Ophelia in the windowseat.[1] Your conversation would please me much more than Shakespeare, and if literature be your resolute bent wouldn't a chapter of *The Brook Kerith* do you as well?

Please to let me know about dinner by wire or telephone.

Always affectionately yours George Moore

28 July 1916   *121 Ebury Street*

My dear Maud,

My sense of gratitude propels me to the writing table to tell you that I am thankful to you for your kindness in inviting me to *Seraglio*. As you said I would, I liked the music better the second time. I walked home exalted but with a regret in my exaltation that I cannot tell Beecham that I appreciated his extraordinary skill in bringing out every shade of colour and every accent. If the dead hear at all, if their ears are not empty, I am sure that Mozart awoke and listened. Madame Nevada sang beautifully in the last act; and I like the tenor, and the bass comedian could not be better. I am again deeply obliged to you— every year my debt goes on increasing, yet you never complain.

Always affectionately yours George Moore

[1] Martin Harvey gave a Shakespeare season at His Majesty's Theatre in May and June 1916.

Saturday [late August or early September 1916][1]

121 Ebury Street

My dear Maud,

I was sorry not to see you. Your message was not given to me correctly and I waited here expecting you. And now I want to see you about the lecture. *The Brook Kerith* seems to have met with sufficient success to justify the lecture, and it might be well to make it plain that the first part of the story is derived from the Gospels. The reviewers do not seem to know that Jesus did not lay claim to divinity in the three synoptic gospels. Our world is the most ignorant of all. Let us try to rub off some of the ignorance. You spoke about this lecture the first; I write to you therefore, but if you are too busy my publisher will attend to it.

When do you return?

Always affectionately yours George Moore

Sunday [24 September 1916]   *121 Ebury Street*

My dear Maud,

Much better than one article would be a set of articles heckling the Bishop of London,[2] three, four maybe. I have noticed that it is the set of articles that counts; the

[1] This letter and the one that follows it are written very shakily, perhaps with the left hand. On 26 August 1916 G.M. wrote to Edmund Gosse: "I am laid up with a broken wrist. Wakened by a violent dream in which I saw the glitter of German banners I precipitated myself forward in the hopes of staying the onset and fell across the hearthrug breaking my wrist badly." *The Brook Kerith* was published on 23 August 1916.

[2] On 25 September 1916 G.M. wrote to John Eglinton: "I am perhaps going to take on the Bishop of London [A. F. Winnington Ingram] in a set of articles [presumably about *The Brook Kerith*], if the newspaper will pay the price I am asking."

92

newspaper gets better value out of the set than out of a single article. This however is a matter for the editor to decide. I am game for one or three—perhaps for six if the articles catch on. Will [you] ask how much the paper is prepared to pay for the articles? I should say twenty pounds an article would not be too much. The articles will be written by me, but I think they should begin by the interviewer putting the question "Sir, we should be glad to hear what you think of these last utterances," that or some more appropriate phrase. On this I break forth.

As ever George Moore

The editor had better write to me if he wants the articles.

[*Typewritten except for first and last lines*]

14 November 1916   *121 Ebury Street*

My dear Maud,
    Were you in the Hall last night and if you were I hope you reached home safely? I was with Mary Hunter who liked all the music equally, but I confess that I do not think anybody ought to play the fiddle for more than a fortnight at a time, and Saint-Saëns is always difficult enough to listen to and more than ever when Ysaye plays him after a piece in five sections consisting mainly of tricks; five sections of tricks are enough without the second lot of tricks.[1]
    Other people's hobbies are always surprising, but

[1] The works played by the orchestra of the Royal Philharmonic Society, conducted by Sir Thomas Beecham, at the Queen's Hall on 13 November 1916, were the Overture to *The Magic Flute*; Debussy's *Images Pour Orchestre*, No. 2; Scene v of Delius's *A Village Romeo and Juliet*; Vivaldi's violin concerto in G Minor; and Saint-Saëns's violin concerto in B minor. Ysaye was the soloist.

93

Beecham's is the oddest, for it would seem that he likes the third act of *Tristan* and the *Siegfried Idyll* diluted with Delius rather than the original versions. It never occurred to me that these works required to be rewritten. The *Romeo and Juliet* is but musical manufacture; I hope never to hear it again; but I cannot think of anything that would give me more pleasure to hear again than the three pieces by Debussy. He is as perfect as antiquity or Mr Pater: one hears genius all the time, and I know of no sensation more delicious: I felt I was listening to music for the first time. The world he opened out to me was as wonderful as Paradise when Adam looked upon it for the first time, and I am writing to ask you to let me know when these three pieces will be given again, for I should not like to miss them.

Always affectionately yours George Moore

[Typewritten except for signature]

12 December 1916   *121 Ebury Street*

My dear Maud,

What has become of you? It is weeks and months since I have seen you or heard from you and the last time we met you were angry with me because I did not like Delius's *Romeo and Juliet*. But there was a time when you did not like it yourself, and Mary Hunter likes the poem as much as she likes the music, yet she does not quarrel with me because the poem seems to me a wooden German effigy.[1] Our likes in art are not dependent on our will. Nancy's poems seem to me on second reading

[1] Frederick Delius's opera *A Village Romeo and Juliet* was first produced in London in 1910. The libretto, written by the composer in German, was based on a story by the Swiss poet Gottfried Keller (1819–90).

94

"Your gain is my loss"

A letter from Henry Tonks to Mrs Hunter, surrendering G.M. to her invitation

much better than they did on a first reading. She has got an exquisite ear for rhythm, and the poems published in *Wheels* vindicate my prophecies pronounced years ago at Holt.[1]

Ever yours George Moore

[?*March 1917*]   *Ritz Hotel*
London

My dear Maud,
    I am leaving Stevenson's book for you, and if you like it it will give me much pleasure to present you with the four volumes. But you may not like it—we get a meaning out of things when they come at the right moment. Stevenson would not have meant much to me twenty-five years ago. You will let me have the volume back, for I should like to keep the copy that stirred my imagination.[2]

Yours ever George Moore

[1] *Wheels* (1916), the first of five annual anthologies of new verse, contained poems by, among others, the three Sitwells and Nancy Cunard. Her seven poems, which included the title-poem "Wheels," were the first of hers to appear in a book.

[2] In his introduction to *Lewis Seymour and Some Women* (published in March 1917) G.M. wrote: "It was only last year that I read *Travels with a Donkey*. Immediately afterwards I read *An Inland Voyage* and my pleasure in this second book was no less than my pleasure in the first." On 8 March 1917 he wrote to Sidney Colvin: "I have to thank you for your edition of Stevenson's letters [4 vols, 1911], which have given me the very greatest pleasure, revealing Stevenson to me even more perfectly than *Travels with a Donkey*, *An Inland Voyage*, *Men and Books*, etc." From this it seems probable that both this letter and G.M.'s revised opinion of Stevenson date from the beginning of 1917, though a letter to John Eglinton of 6 January 1914 suggests that G.M. had already begun to appreciate Stevenson by then.

Thursday [*1918*]   *121 Ebury Street*

Dearest Maud,

It is always a pleasure to me to do anything you ask me to do. I am therefore leaving at your house a water-colour by Steer[1] to be sold at the sale you are interested in.

As ever George Moore

Saturday [*1918*]   *121 Ebury Street*

My dear Maud,

What about the cheese you promised to get for me? Do get it for I'm in need of something to eat.

As ever George Moore

Tonks was shocked when I told him I had given away a Steer water-colour. I could see that he perceived in me one who had sinned against the Holy Ghost. I saw Mrs Dudley and was introduced to Lord Curzon's eldest daughter and was impressed by her intelligent demeanour. When you see Lord Curzon, will you ask him what he is going to do with Cologne, if it is to be spared, and if the war will end without our having a single Cathedral to our credit.[2]

G.M.

[*?1918*]   *121 Ebury Street*

My dear Maud,

The lines themselves have no value for me, and I omit them without a pang—a permit goes to the printer tonight that he may distribute the type. You asked me

---

[1] Philip Wilson Steer (1860-1924), the artist, was a close friend of G.M.'s for forty years.

[2] George Nathaniel, first Marquess Curzon of Kedleston (1859-1925), was at this time Lord President of the Council.

often to dedicate a book to you. I did my best but somehow I am unable to think in conventional phrases. I
should have asked Lord Curzon to write it.[1]

Always affectionately yours George Moore

[*Postscript torn off*]

[*?April 1919*]   *121 Ebury Street*

My dear Maud,
   I couldn't resist your influence any longer, for my life
had begun to seem very murk. Oh light of my life, I hope
brightened soon again.

As ever George Moore

17 April 1919   *121 Ebury Street*

Dearest Maud,
   I went to the opera hoping to see you and *Figaro*, but
the attendant footman told me that *Figaro* was played in
the afternoon and that you were not coming as the opera
was *Madame Butterfly*, so I left before the performance.
Since that evening I have come from the Albert Hall,[2]
Oxford whither I went to see the Ruskin drawings and
was much gratified. The little picture gallery possesses a
singularly beautiful Rossetti, a very early one done before
he fell into mannerisms, a group of people coming upon
Dante drawing an angel in a window. The gesture of the

[1] It is impossible to say which book of G.M.'s this refers to, but
it may well have been *A Storyteller's Holiday*, which was published
in 1918 without a dedication. The reference to Lord Curzon seems to
support this date. Moreover, the Uniform Edition of this book did
contain a dedication to Lady Cunard (see note, p. 165).

[2] A gigantic slip of the pen for Ashmolean Museum, to which
Ruskin presented his drawings in 1860. The Rossetti picture, "Dante
drawing an Angel on the Anniversary of Beatrice's Death" (1853),
was acquired by the Ashmolean in 1894.

man coming forward could not be better and Dante awakens slowly from his revery at the touch of his friend's arm thrown about his shoulder. A woman stands by an ecclesiastic swooning with expectation. If one is to have drama in a picture we get it in this picture and the drama is of the kind worth having—spiritual drama. The scene takes place between two windows—we have a view of the city on the right, and on the left a green landscape that Pissarro might have painted. The swooning profile and the deep blue cloak lined with green silk are exquisite craft and vision. The Ruskin drawings testify to the world's mistake and to his own mistake—he was a tiresome writer whose genius went into drawing. And now about another thing—I enclose a letter that appeared in *The Times* today.[1] It might be well to send it to Lord Curzon—he should see it, for the way indicated is the only way. I am going to Mary Hunter's tomorrow. I wish that you were.

As ever, my dearest memory, George Moore

[*April-May 1919*]   *121 Ebury Street*

Dearest Maud,

You said something at the opera about Lord Curzon having spoken of my letter to *The Times* as being an attack on the government policy—a marvellous criticism if you understood him, for my letter is merely a develop-

[1] Headed "Ireland: a Solution", this letter of G.M.'s advocated the economic development of Ireland by means of the construction of a naval dockyard in Galway and a tunnel between Ireland and the mainland. In the Epistle Dedicatory to T. W. Rolleston in the 1920 edition of *Esther Waters*, G.M. referred to "yester-year, when we were engaged in trying to wheedle the English public into accepting the only solution (yours) of the Irish Difficulty—a line of railway linking a western harbour with a northern tunnel joining Ireland to Scotland . . . letters that you wrote and that I signed".

ment of Lord French's speech at Belfast [on] August 5th, 1918. I have written a long article—*un article de fond*—for the *Sunday Chronicle*;[1] do get the paper, for I think this article is among my best. You will see that I refer, without mentioning any name *of course*, to Lord Curzon's criticism. I should have thought that my letter would have fallen in with Lord Curzon's ideas and that of all men he would have been the most likely to approve of my *Times* letter. In this world one is sure of nothing. You will be able to judge when you have seen my article if it would be worth while to call his attention to it.

Most affectionately yours George Moore

[*July 1919*][2]

Hotel Roblin
Rue Chauveau-Lagarde
Paris

Dearest Maud,

According to plan I took the boat from Southampton to St Malo, but found it impossible—nearly impossible—to get from St Malo to Nantes. It took two days, and at Rennes I and a young woman (a travelling acquaintance) found ourselves stranded at one o'clock in the morning. We went in search of an hotel, but none was open, and we spent six hours in a railway carriage. The episode was platonic. At Nantes I visited Le Pallet and found some ruins and a kindly *Curé* who knew all about Héloïse and Abélard and explained the ruins to me. I followed the pretty river in a sousing downpour, dreaming of the lovers of long ago in a boat under the willows and poplars, the

---

[1] "My Irish Solution" (*Sunday Chronicle*, 4 May 1919) again advocated a tunnel between Ireland and the mainland.

[2] On 17 January 1920 G.M. wrote to Dujardin: "I went to France last July on the trail of Héloïse and Abélard . . . I have found nothing but a few ruins in a little town called Le Pallet, near Nantes."

descendants of the trees that sheltered from sun and rain the rare birds of the renaissance. The picture gallery at Nantes contains some fine sculpture, twelfth, thirteenth and fourteenth century, a virgin whose celestial serenity contrasted with King Solomon's terrestrial melancholy. Two landscapes by Oudry remain fixed in my memory, and a lady in a purple dress by Ingres. I spent two days at Tours remembering the grey and green landscape of the Loire interspersed with yellow sandy reaches—a birdless river. No heron lifts his long grey neck, a watchful bird, thane of the shallows, and flops away on unwieldy wings. Nor did I catch sight of ducks or moorhen; but at Blois swallows were about in thousands, wearying the eyes with swift curving flight high up in the blue air and skimming over the surface of the languid river. The fishermen watch their floats from the beautiful bridge with a patience that is not mine nor thine, dear Maud. When shall I see thee? When wilt thou accept an humble dinner in 121 Ebury Street and give the pleasure of hearing and seeing thee, the only one that remains to me?

You must come to me. At 44 Grosvenor Square there are people about that are of no interest to me, as little intelligent they seem as squeaking dolls: excellent folk, no doubt, but I have lost my taste for them, that is all.

Most affectionately yours George Moore

Tuesday night [*19 August 1919*]   *121 Ebury Street*

My dear Maud,

I beg you to believe that I appreciate your kindness asking me to luncheon on Friday. Could I come I would, but I'm composing every morning from ten to two, sometimes till three. My only free day is Sunday, and next Sunday I have arranged to go to Richmond to see

Sir Somebody Cook's pictures.[1] Will you tell Nancy that I should like to see her and hope she'll find it convenient to call here soon, for I should like to talk to her about her poem which in my opinion is a great advance on her other work.

Always affectionately yours George Moore

What a splendid article Newman contributed to the *Observer*, "Lord Berners' Crucifixion".[2] It is the only real piece of criticism that has appeared in the English language for many years. *Avowals* will be distributed during the first week in September.

13 September [*1919*]   *121 Ebury Street*

Dearest Maud,

I enclose the *Chesterian* for the sake of my article "The Nineness in the Oneness" which isn't very good but may interest you all the same.[3] Newman's writing in the *Observer* was as good as ever and he saw below the surface —he is the only one who does. That which captures the admiration of the public at once passes away quickly; there are no exceptions to this rule in ancient or modern times; if there were, human nature would be quite different from what it is. We must be always on our guard. By

[1] Sir Frederick Cook's collection at Doughty House, Richmond. G.M. used this same phrase in a letter to Gosse, clearly written on the same day and postmarked 19 August 1919.

[2] On 13 July 1919 Ernest Newman published in the *Observer* an uncomplimentary notice of Lord Berners's piano piece, *Le Poisson D'Or*. On 10 August Lord Berners protested in a letter, and on 17 August Newman renewed his onslaught in an article headed "The Modern Creed".

[3] This article on the interdependence of the arts, with particular reference to Wagner, appeared in the *Chesterian* (a music periodical edited by G. Jean Aubry) in September 1919 and in the *Century Magazine* for November.

the way, Newman's article contained some argument that it would be easy to pierce.

I hope I shall see you this week, for the hours I pass in your society are the only ones that leave any impression on my mind. I have finished the second act and have thought of a title: *The Coming of Gabrielle*. It would be better in French: *Gabrielle s'annonce*.[1]

Always affectionately yours George Moore

Wednesday night [September 1919]

Dearest Maud,

I have managed to secure a copy of *Avowals* for you and will write in it the inscription that collected in my head as I drove home: "For Maud, the incarnate Spring, whom I love as the goats love the spring." I don't know if you would like this inscription. It may hap that you will let me know.[2]

As ever George Moore

Wednesday night. Or is it Tuesday?   *121 Ebury Street*
[5 November 1919]

Dearest Maud,

It is most kind of you to think of me, most kind; but nobody in the world is as kind [as you] and nobody in the world as appreciative as I.

I shall look forward to seeing you tomorrow night at the opera. I look forward to *Falstaff*.[3]

Most affectionately yours George Moore

[1] See notes, pp. 33 and 126.
[2] See note 2, p. 104.
[3] Of the twelve performances of Verdi's *Falstaff* which were given at Covent Garden between 1911 and 1933 the only Thursday one was on 6 November 1919, and I have dated this and the following letter accordingly.

Dearest Maud,

I hope to see you soon and to see you well. I spent a very interesting evening listening to *Falstaff* and meditating during the acts on what I had heard—a mode of enjoyment foreign to the other habitants of the box, who seized on the interval to babble: "And do you know his sister? The one who married so and so. It was at Rome when etc." Jane Churchill came in to discourse on art, and her notion of art seemed to be that it was very meritorious for a writer to change his style. "Just fancy, and he over seventy when he changed", to which I answered "You are quite right, it is written in the style of a man who has just changed his style." But she did not see the irony. We have only to think of *Pelléas* to apprehend the Italian vulgarity of Verdi; very like Dickens; yet there are good things in it. The Italian Ambassador admired the fugue in the last act; and in self-defence I asked him if he liked the fugue in *The Mastersingers*. "In *The Mastersingers* the fugue is in the second act, but in *Falstaff* it is in the last act," he answered. But when shall I see you? And has Nancy come home? If she has, tell her I want to see her.

Always affectionately yours George Moore

10 July [1920]   *121 Ebury Street*

My dear Maud,

I sent you *Esther Waters* (new edition) to remind you of your girlhood—a certain shot-silk dress among other things, and in the hope that it would provoke you to writing to me, to coming here or to inviting me to come to you. But *Esther* has done none of these things and I have begun to think that you did not like the words written on the flyleaf. Yet in my memory they seem harmless enough.[1]

Do write to your affectionate old friend

George Moore

[26] October 1920   5 Carlton House Terrace
                                       S.W.1.

My dear,

One more copy of the six *Avowals* that lost their signature plates and cannot be sold without an attestation from me to this effect remains, and as I have not given you anything for a long time I should like to give you my last Avowal just as I gave you my first. Will you pay me a visit tomorrow, Wednesday, and we will inscribe it befittingly together?[2] I am going to spend the week-end with Mary Hunter and shall leave London on Friday.

As ever yours George Moore

[?1 November 1920][3]   [121 Ebury Street]

My dear Maud,

Of course I was disappointed at not being able to see you. You would not have it otherwise, would you?

My interest in 5 Carlton House Terrace is centred in you and not in the people who come there. It may hap that you'd like to see me one of these days and you would

[1] This inscribed copy has disappeared. The new edition of *Esther Waters* was published in June 1920, and in a limited edition in October.

[2] The inscription reads: "To Lady Cunard. Time, the arch thief, has not robbed me of my soul, my affection for you, dear Maud. Yours always, George Moore. October 30, 1920."

[3] Both G.M. and Cora Lady Strafford stayed with Mrs Hunter at Hill Hall for the week-end of 29 October to 1 November 1920. Moreover, Lady Cunard had just rented 5 Carlton House Terrace, where she lived till 1925, when she moved to 7 Grosvenor Square.

do well to come here. The last time you came Josephine[1] was here unfortunately. But this will not happen again. Cora[2] was one of Mary Hunter's guests and she talked for three quarters [of an hour] after every meal, and we all sat wilting in our chairs, overpowered by a volubility that has laid three husbands in their graves, to say nothing of forty-three thousand ducks and twenty-seven thousand geese—Tom's bag, so she told us, during the six years that he spent in Cashmere. And when that country was reft of feathers he had to return, but the thought of Cora's tongue was too much, and he died as you know on the voyage home. Cora should apply her money to the raising of a cenotaph to the bipeds, unfeathered and feathered.

Always affectionately yours George Moore

7 December [*1920*]   *121 Ebury Street*

Dearest Maud,

You brought into the world a hard heart as well as much beauty, grace and charm, and it is small wonder that I fell in love with you, remained in love with you, and always shall love you. Your party last night was animated with your personality and everybody was inspired with an unwonted happiness. I enjoyed myself quietly for I met many friends and acquaintances, and all were smiling and agreeable, magnetised by you, for you charm even the morose. Even one to whom I seemed guilty of rudeness once, through your fault, came and sat down

[1] Lady Cunard's American friend Mrs Marshall, who had participated in the accident at Munich in 1910 (see pp. 78–80).

[2] Cora Lady Strafford (*d.* 1932) was an American by birth. Originally Cora Smith, she married (1) Samuel Colgate, of New York; (2) the fourth Earl of Strafford (1831–99); (3) Martyn Thomas Kennard (1859–1920), who spent a great part of his life shooting big game in the East.

beside me, forgave me, accepted my explanation, which he wouldn't have done, I am certain, if your presence hadn't purified the atmosphere of all bitterness, quelling animosities old and new. I only rued my shyness which prevented me from making a matter clear to the Prince of Wales which might be of use to him, but as you will doubtless see him within the next few days you'll be able to do what I failed to do. Perhaps you will be good enough to read him a portion of this letter.

The reason of all this Irish discontent is a sentimental one. The Irish feel themselves to be in a northern island out of the path of civilisation, neglected, and looked upon with contumely by the rest of Europe. There is no real republicanism in Ireland; the Irish are a hieratic people, loving class distinctions and ceremonial; and if the Prince of Wales were to go to live there for two or three months of the year Sinn Fein would pass out of sight quickly. The Prince likes hunting and he'd get the finest hunting in the world in Meath. The foxes are stronger than the English foxes and the galloping better. He would acquire an unprecedented popularity, one which would make the popularity he won in Australia and America seem as water is to wine, if he were to show some sympathy for national aspirations. I do not mean political aspirations; he would not allude to politics, nor is there any need, for it would be easy for him to awaken enthusiasm by allusion to Irish history, the brighter parts of it, and of all to say some words about the Irish language —that it was well that the Irish wished to preserve their language; and if he learnt a few words of Irish, enough to bring into a speech, the whole country would follow him. The Prince has the gift of popularity and the Irish are waiting for somebody to love. There are always reactions and they have hated till they are weary of hating. I should have liked to develop this theme last night but a ballroom is hardly a suitable place and I was shy and embarrassed. But perhaps you'll speak to the Prince on this subject and read these lines to him. Or if you think a better plan would be to invite me to luncheon to meet him I shall be very pleased of course. Of this there can be no doubt, that he is the one who can settle the Irish question.

Always affectionately yours George Moore

7 *December* [1920]   *121 Ebury Street*

Dearest Maud,

I wrote you a longish and somewhat (perhaps) important letter this morning, and I am writing now to beg you to push this matter forward. Help will come from some side—the riddle will be unriddled, but nobody knows by whom.

If you are not likely to see the Prince for some days you might copy out that portion of my letter which concerns him and send it to him for his consideration. Ireland is not as dangerous as India. If the project were carried through with skill, Sinn Fein would be sponged off the slate in three weeks and less. Of course it will be said that this is not the moment. To my thinking it is just the moment. Give your mind to my letter, that is all I ask: I am confident you have the necessary skill.

Always affectionately yours George Moore

22 *December* [*Postmark 1920*]   *121 Ebury Street*

My dear Maud,

You were often kind enough to say that you would like me to dedicate a book to you; I should like to very much indeed, and *Héloïse and Abélard* is a work detached from things of the day, it is written with more reticence

than many of my books and is probably as good as anything I have written. Will you have it? Please let me know
as soon as possible, for the first volume will go to the
binders at once.

Always affectionately yours George Moore

23 December [Postmark 1920]   121 Ebury Street

My dear Maud,

I am delighted to hear that you contemplate coming
to see me on Saturday. I wish you would lunch here; you
shall have all that you dare to eat. If you cannot I shall
look forward to seeing you in the afternoon—after three
o'clock. Do not disappoint me. Thank you for sending a
copy of my letter to the Prince.

Always affectionately yours George Moore

26 December [Postmark 1920]   121 Ebury Street

My dear Maud,

I have given my mind to the perplexing question of
the dedication which is a subtle commentary on the
affections. The thought expressed is subtle and the expression is subtle and I have never heard of refined and
subtle thinking provoking vulgar remarks. Colonel
Repington and Mrs Asquith were much criticised for
their vulgarities. I do not mean that Colonel Repington
and Mrs Asquith are themselves vulgarians, but not being
writers, not being possessed of the craft of writing, they
appear as vulgarians in their memoirs.[1]

I enclose a copy of the dedication. Read it and let me
know what you wish done with it. I cannot publish it

[1] Colonel Repington's *Diary* was published in 1920. Margot
Asquith's *Autobiography* did not appear in book form till 1922, but
portions of it had been serialised in the press.

without your permission and if you read it carefully you will see that it cannot be altered. Do not show it around, do not ask advice, for advice is never very wise; we have to judge everything for ourselves. If you show it to anybody the story of the dedication will run round London and in three days three new stories will be in circulation. All your fears will be realised and there will be no text to give the lie to the rumours.

Always affectionately yours George Moore

P.S. I must know within the next couple of days, to-morrow if possible, for the press is waiting.

30 December [Postmark 1920]　　　　*121 Ebury Street*

Dearest Maud,

I have written to the printer and before you get this letter the type will be distributed. And now that the question is purely academic let me laugh or at least smile at your adviser's dilemma—how could the family lawyer give you different advice? In Buckmaster's place I should have given you exactly the same advice. The dedication was a bit of eighteenth-century gallantry and would have been admired by Lord Buckmaster if he had not been called to give advice in his professional capacity. But it does not really matter. My thoughts are what matter and you know that I always have and always shall love you.

Always affectionately yours George Moore

P.S. In what you said about the stories in *The Untilled Field* you showed more discrimination than all the critics. The stories every one, with the possible exception of *The Wild Goose*, match the stories you mention. I am sorry *The Lake* is not in the volume.

5 January 1921   *Hill Hall*
                                       Theydon Mount
                                              Epping
My dear Maud,

Before coming here I struggled to suppress my feelings in many epistles dedicatory but with indifferent success from the point of view of the family solicitor, for in every one he would have detected traces of my affection for you. Nor would his discoveries be altogether imaginary, for when I think of you words will not obey me, and after a little while begin to catch a tinge of the essential instinct in me—you. You will find it hard to understand this, and an explanation would but darken the mystery still further, no other life having passed into your life and become part of you. It really is most strange, for I tried for nearly two days to detach myself from you and write the conventional letter, but could not finish one without resort to a turn of phrase that would not have met with the family solicitor's approval—yours perhaps but not his; his business being to safeguard himself.

I regret my failure deeply, for very often as we sat talking literature together it seemed to me that I caught sight of the wish to read your name on the front page of some book of mine hovering in your eyes. But masterpieces are alone commemorative, and it is not likely that *Héloïse and Abélard* is one, masterpieces being as rare in art as great passions are in life.

Always affectionately yours George Moore

Wednesday, 16 February [1921]   *121 Ebury Street*
My dear Maud,

I have (according to your instructions) omitted your

name from the dedication of *Héloïse and Abélard* but trust to your indiscretion.[1]

Always affectionately yours George Moore

Saturday [5 March 1921][2]   *Hill Hall*
                                             Theydon Mount
                                                  Epping

My dear Maud,
    I shall be so pleased to hear from you again that you will not be able to postpone writing to me any longer. And with increasing expectancy I shall look forward to hearing from you during the forthcoming week. Shall you be in Paris in April? I hope so, for though I am longing to get a letter I long still more to see you. I hope you liked the article I wrote about Nancy's book.[3] Everybody I met during the week spoke to me about it, writers, publishers and friends. Mary Hunter thought that I mingled praise with admonition most skilfully. You sent the article on to Nancy of course. Nancy wrote thanking me for the letter I wrote about her poems—a

[1] The published dedication to the first edition of *Héloïse and Abélard* (1921) runs:

A Madame X

Héloïse et Abélard fut composé pour célébrer mon amour. Les épreuves sont corrigées, les brouillons au panier, l'encrier est à sec. Erreur! J'en tire une dernière goutte et avec une plume estropiée je vous écris cette petite épitre dédicatoire. Je vous prie de l'accepter, Madame, sans trop me chicaner sur un mot qui semblera trop fort à certains sots, pauvres êtres, qui voudraient remplacer le mot amour par celui d'amitié, ne sachant pas que le cœur ne connaît que l'amour. G.M.

In the Uniform Edition (1925) the dedication was omitted.

[2] G.M. signed the Hill Hall visitors book on 6 March.

[3] G.M.'s long review of Nancy Cunard's first book of poems, *Outlaws*, appeared in the *Observer* on 27 February 1921.

most enthusiastic letter; I never knew Nancy as moved before, and I should like to hear how she liked the article, which of course was better than the letter of a man who is by no means a letter-writer.

Mary Hunter sends you her love, mine you have had always and will have it to the end.

Always affectionately yours George Moore

27 March [Postmark 1921]   121 Ebury Street

Dearest Maud,

I am going to Paris on the 4th and hope to see you and we'll talk over your project of going into business with a view to increasing your income which the double tax reduces terribly. I am afraid that neither you nor I will ever make money in business: there is a great deal of money to be made in tailoring, but do you think that we should get any share of it if we set up a shop in George Street, Hanover Square? Would it not be better to avoid the double tax by living half the year in France and half in London?

I am glad you liked the review I wrote about Nancy's book but am puzzled, for you say "some parts of your review." You surely do not think it should have been all praise? The faults I mentioned were mentioned for I wished the review to read like a genuine expression of opinion.

Always affectionately yours George Moore

P.S. You never write to me and I fear that my long love story is dropping into a sad draggletail.

Why did you listen to the foolish family solicitor, for Buckmaster is no better; mentally he is one. I never wrote anything better than the dedication, and my pen does not

err. I have told nobody but will still continue to rely on
your indiscretion.

G.M.

15 May [?1921]   *121 Ebury Street*
Dearest Maud,
   I have been working month after month, long days of
six or seven hours, looking forward to seeing you—*une
bonne bouche à la fin de la journée.* So Nancy has gone south,
and as you say I shall miss her. But I shall be in Paris till
July, and perhaps she will have returned—her journeys are
short ones. I shall write and give her my address.
   With much love and affection George Moore

Friday [Postmark 8 July 1921]   *121 Ebury Street*
My dear Maud,
   I hope that you will be able to come here to see your
beautiful present in my drawing room. I had a handsome
bowl (crescent mark) and you have no idea of what a
fine show they make together. My visits to you are not
real visits, but a vain simulacrum of your visits here ages
ago. It must be a year since you crossed my threshold. Of
course I know by this time that it is no part of your
pleasure to see me hanging on to your words; your
instinct was to love not to inspire love; to be loved bored
you, and when the inevitable happed you passed on to
another chapel to enter a new set of devotions. But just
once, before you leave London, you might sacrifice
yourself, submit yourself to my peaceful adoration. The
later epigram in the *Observer* was very poor, I tried
several but epigrams will not be hurried.[1]
   Ave Faustina plena gratia immortales ago tibi gratias is

[1] On 26 June 1921 the *Observer* published an article by G.M.,
couched in the form of an interview, called "The Tenth Muse,"

better, and I am glad the epigram missed fire in the *Observer*, for it is more to the point in a letter thanking you for the Worcester china.

Always affectionately yours Gauslin[1]

Hail Faustina full of grace, [I] give thee eternal thanks.

21 August [*1921*]   *121 Ebury Street*

An hour's talk with you alone, dearest Maud, brings all my love of you back again; an inexpressible joy, a drenching sadness it is, and all that is most essential and real in me.

I enclose the *Fragments from Héloïse and Abélard*[2] and write "as ever," feeling that the words cut to the centre when I address them to you.

George Moore

27 September [*Postmark 1921*]   *121 Ebury Street*

Dearest Maud,

It would give me a great deal of pleasure to get a line from you telling me how you are and how Nancy is, and how the case is going. You are both bad correspondents and I do not hope to change you into irrepressible letter-writers, but it would give an old friend, who loves you, much pleasure to get a note from you, that is all.

The same as ever George Moore

---

concerning the Phoenix Society and its productions of sixteenth- and seventeenth-century plays. The "interview" ended with G.M.'s saying: "Let us be grateful to the Phoenix, risen from the ashes of Opera, and cry as we pass in and out of the theatre: 'Ave, Faustina, grato animo te salutamus'."

[1] I cannot explain this signature, unless it is a wild mis-spelling of Gaucelm (see p. 194).

[2] A pamphlet privately printed in 1921 and containing revisions to *Héloïse and Abélard.*

Dearest Maud,

I am sorry indeed to hear that you were ill. I began to suspect illness and would have gone to inquire if I had not found your note when I returned home. I will call tomorrow at 5.30 or six o'clock. A woman who is coming to London for 'another operation' begged me to let her come to tea. For some reason that neither she nor I can fathom she takes great pleasure in my company, and she says it will give her courage to get her appendicitis out. God knows all this is foolish enough, but we live in a world in which we must shrink from thinking, else we do nothing, all action seeming folly. The eastern philosophers discovered this long and long ago. I do not suppose that she will stay more than an hour, so I see no reason why I should not be with you at 5.30 or 6. *I will try.*

Always affectionately yours George Moore

[*? late 1921*]

Dearest Maud,

I am longing to see you, and the longing is deeper than your longing to see me. I was very nearly calling to see you yesterday at three o'clock, and very nearly going to the Ritz to see you today at the same time, but feared to intrude. I will come to luncheon tomorrow, Monday, but the Venice trip is impossible. I have too much to do. The actress who is going to produce *Gabrielle* has gone to France.[1] She returns on Friday and I must see her.

Affectionately yours George Moore

[1] This almost certainly refers to the actress-producer Auriol Lee, whose plans for the production of the play in New York came to nothing.

Sunday [? *1921*]   *121 Ebury Street*

My dear Maud,

I hope you have not forgotten that you said you would lunch here on Tuesday. I shall expect you if I do not hear from you that something untoward prevents you from coming. In that case I shall be disappointed. According to arrangement I am to read you Landor's dialogue, which I hope will be spoken on the stage the day *The Coming of Gabrielle* is given—the reading will take about twelve minutes.[1] Afterwards we go to the Tate, I believe.

Always affectionately yours George Moore

Friday night [*Postmark 22 October 1921*]

My dear Maud,

I enjoyed my afternoon shopping with you, oh woman of infinite variety, and it would give me much pleasure to go to see the pictures with you tomorrow, but I promised Mrs Harter to remain at home to see her. She is coming to speak to me about her novel *A Love Conference*.[2]

Always affectionately yours George Moore

Don't forget Dulwich[3] on Tuesday.

Tuesday night [? *November 1921*]   *121 Ebury Street*

Dearest Maud,

When are you going to take me out again? To Selfridge's or to Dulwich, which? I dined last night in the company of

---

[1] Landor was one of G.M.'s favourite authors, but there is no record of which dialogue he was referring to, nor was it read from the stage.

[2] This novel by Mrs Arthur Harter (neé Ethel Maud de Fonblanque) was published in April 1922.

[3] The picture gallery there, which played an important part in *Evelyn Innes*.

some Americans of the joyous kind—the kind that comes to Europe, and they were surprised, amazed is the word, that you should go to Selfridge's and with me! With me of all people in the world; and they seemed to find it hard, nay impossible, to associate either of us with Selfridge's, but that we should have gone to Selfridge's together seemed beyond the reach of their imagination. I gave some frivolous answer, not the answer that trembled on my lips—discretion forbade it. I would follow Lady Cunard, I was minded to say, to Selfridge's end, and as Mary Stuart said she would follow Bothwell: you know in what costume she proposed to pursue him, of course you do. You have read the Casket Letters.[1]

> Always affectionately yours George Moore

17 November [?1921]   *121 Ebury Street*

Dearest Maud,

This is to remind you that you promised to call here on Saturday after luncheon to take me to Dulwich. I hope you will not stay to entertain the guests with your wonderful spirits and wit, for in November the days are thin and shortlived.

> With the same affection George Moore

21 November [Postmark 1921]   *121 Ebury Street*

My dear Maud,

What have I done to merit this outburst of generosity? I cannot think nor am I inclined to give much time to the thinking of the cause, so pleased am I at the thought of

[1] It was not in the Casket Letters, but in a letter from Kirkcaldy of Grange to the Earl of Bedford dated 20 April 1567, that Mary was reported as saying that she "sall go with him [Bothwell] to the worldes ende in ane white peticote or she leve him" (Scottish Calendar, ii, 322).

seeing you again. I will come to luncheon with pleasure (delight) on Friday, and call to see you on Wednesday if you do not call for me. Dulwich would interest you, I'm sure—the wonderful Rubens, and you owe Dulwich a visit.

Always affectionately yours George Moore

9 December [Postmark 1921]　　　　　　*121 Ebury Street*

My dear Maud,

If you propose to take me out driving it will be much better that you call here for me, I shall be ready waiting. Last time I went to fetch you visitor after visitor came in and we never got away. I was sorry not to be at your dance, but all that day I was writing an article about Paul to be read on Christmas Day showing him to be the author of the Acts, and the composition was so difficult that I forgot your dance. If I had remembered it I would have abandoned Paul cheerfully, Lydia, Priscilla and Eunice to boot.[1]

Always affectionately George Moore

Wednesday [? 14 December 1921]　　　　　*121 Ebury Street*

Dearest Maud,

I was disappointed that our drive together fell through but I was glad to see you brightening as usual the lives of dull people. A charming spectacle that is, and [in] the passing in review [of] the season's folk you remember that the conversation turned on the beauty of women's hands. I wrote some verses on a pair of hands that will never pass out of my memory. I send them to you though you hate French verses:

---

[1] See *The Acts of the Apostles*, chaps. xvi and xviii.

Souvenir d'une Visite
Je vois tes mains dans ma pensée—
Jeunes mains, fleurs de la rosée.
Je vois ta main gauche posée
Comme par Ingres sur ton sein,
Et j'entrevois le beau dessin
Qu'il aurait fait d'après ta main.[1]
Always affectionately yours George Moore

Saturday [24 December 1921]   *[121 Ebury Street]*
My dear Maud,
    You have not sent me Nancy's poem nor have you
asked me to come to see you. Nor have you ordered your
car to stop at my door. I hope the old year will not pass
away without my seeing you again.
    Tomorrow you will find an article in the *Sunday Times*
claiming Paul as the author of the Acts.[2]
              Always affectionately yours George Moore

26 December [1921][3]   *121 Ebury Street*
    I waited all day for you and the morning seemed
long and the afternoon still longer. Till six I did not
lose hope and after six I re-read your card. It is true
that you wrote "Do write to me, I'll see you on
Monday", but I did not connect the two sentences.
You always end your letters with "Do write to me,"

    [1] G.M. sent a copy of these verses to Gosse on 9 December 1921 and
to Dujardin on 26 December. To Gosse he commented: "I suppose
they must be bad, but the hands that provoked them are the beautifullest—the Honourable Mrs Fellowes' hands."
    [2] G.M.'s article "Works of St. Paul" appeared in the *Sunday Times*
on 25 December 1921.
    [3] This letter was in the same envelope as the one of 9 December
and written on the same paper, so I have placed it in the same year.

and the words are always welcome like "the rosy fingers of the dawn" and "the grey-eyed Athene" and the residue are welcome in Homer. I did not think that "Do write to me" was anything more than your constantly recurring phrase, part of your style. So it was that I missed seeing you this afternoon and so it is that I am sad this evening.

As ever George Moore

29 January 1922   *121 Ebury Street*

Dearest Maud,

I cannot endure life very long without seeing and hearing you, and I returned home deliciously refreshed, as I might from a fountain to dream again. You appear as I sit thinking my stories, and it is sometimes your white hands that I remember, sometimes it is your joyous spirituality that enraptures me; and very often I fall on my knees and thank God for his great mercy in having made you known to me.

As ever George Moore

Gold wings across the sea!
Grey light from tree to tree,
Gold hair beside my knee,
I pray thee come to me,
Gold wings!

The water slips,
The red-bill'd moorhen dips
Sweet kisses on red lips;
Alas! the red rust grips,
And the blood-red dagger rips,
Yet, O knight, come to me!

Are not my blue eyes sweet?
The west wind from the wheat
Blows cold across my feet;
Is it not time to meet
Gold wings across the sea?

White swans on the green moat,
Small feathers left afloat
By the blue-painted boat;
Swift running of the stoat,
Sweet gurgling note by note
Of sweet music.

O gold wings,
Listen how gold hair sings,
And the Ladies Castle rings,
Gold wings across the sea.

I sit on a purple bed,
Outside, the wall is red,

etc. etc.[1]

14 February [Postmark 1922]   *121 Ebury Street*

My dear Maud,
    I was sorry I could not come to luncheon on Monday
and the afternoon I spent at home forcibly, the dentist
having absorbed my energies for the day. All my 'copy'
has gone to the printer and before settling down to edit
my works for the final edition I am going away to France,
to the South, that I have never seen: Orange and Arles and
Montauban famous because of Ingres. I look forward to
seeing Nancy.
            Always affectionately yours George Moore

[1] An extract from "Golden Wings" by William Morris (from *The
Defence of Guenevere*, 1858). It was one of G.M.'s favourite poems and
he included the whole of it in his anthology *Pure Poetry* (1924).

Saturday [*April–May 1922*]   *Hôtel Restaurant Foyot*
                                          Paris

Dearest Maud,
    Your card with a few words written upon it was for-
warded. Some of the words were illegible but I read that
you were sorry to miss me, for which expression of good-
will accept my best thanks.
    I am leaving for Fontainebleau tomorrow and Nancy
leaves tomorrow for London. My address will be: Le Val
Changis, Avon, Seine-et-Marne for the next month. The
first thing I shall do will be to apply myself to the composition of the preface to my collected works, and this
preface will not be the usual tasteless flummery. I have an
idea for a preface; and idea is a good thing—a good pre-
paration for writing.[1]
                Always affectionately yours George Moore

Friday [*Postmark 10 June 1922*]   *121 Ebury Street*

Dearest Maud,
    I am heartbroken. I never see you nor do I hear from
you. Do not ask me to come to Carlton House Terrace
for you have visitors always. But do you come here.
                With the same affection George Moore

11 June [*Postmark 1922*]   *121 Ebury Street*

My dear Maud,
    It is very kind of you to ask me to luncheon, and I
regret that weariness of mind and body prevents me from
accepting your invitation. The few who care to see me

    [1] The Carra Edition of G.M.'s works was published in a limited
edition in America, 1922–24. The preface to the first volume is called
Apologia pro Scriptis Meis. See note, p. 51.

must come here, for I am overworn; the burden of work seems to increase year by year.

With the same affection George Moore

[*Postmark of receipt 9 August 1922*]   *Netherton Hall*
Honiton
S. Devon

My dear Maud,
I have nothing to say but I'm thinking of you and so I write to say nothing in particular; in fact my only news is that there are more beautiful churches in this part of the country than elsewhere. I visited three yesterday and all three are "riveted and screwed upon my mind".

Always affectionately yours despite your negligence
George Moore

[*Registered letter*]   *121 Ebury Street*
18 August [*Postmark 1922*]

I believe you will understand when I tell you that I was thinking of one thing only—the Diploma Gallery[1] which I hoped to show you. It closes early and the talk seemed unlikely to stop. It is possible that in my weariness I said something you thought the company might misinterpret; a few words would have been enough to make my meaning clear, that the purest girl in the world might hesitate to demand her freedom if the suit were contested. But you blew up like a hurricane.

Always affectionately yours George Moore

[*19 or 20 August 1922*]   *121 Ebury Street*
My dear Maud,
Your letter took a great weight of sorrow and dismay from off my mind, and I am quite willing to admit that

1 In Burlington House.

123

my refusal to join in the conversation was unseemly. I do not plead the excuse that I could think of nothing but my appointment with you to go to see the pictures, but I do beg you to believe in my sincere repentance and that come what may I shall never offend again. And it is a great relief to gather from your letter that my unseemly conduct was the cause of your misunderstanding some words of mine about Nancy. But why do [you] say we shall meet "somewhere" soon? Why do you not come here? Old men may be visited surely, even by the circumspect.

Affectionately yours George Moore

19 April [*1923*]   *121 Ebury Street*

My dear Maud,

My publisher in America is pressing me unduly for corrected copies of my books for his uniform edition and were I to accept your invitation to luncheon I should miss another mail. Tomorrow, Friday, will be mail day. Moreover I have to finish another Conversation before I go to Paris. The new Conversation is with Granville-Barker, about a national theatre, and I give you credit, as far as I am able, for the great services you have rendered to art and in terms which will meet with your approval.[1]

Always affectionately yours George Moore

[1] *Conversations in Ebury Street* (1924), chap. xviii:

Granville-Barker. Lady Cunard takes an important part in your deliberations.

Moore. She is our President. The Phoenix owed three hundred pounds, but at one of the last performances the announcement was made that a benefactor or a benefactress, who did not wish his or her name to be known, had paid the debt. I hasten to say that I do not attribute the paying of the debt to Lady Cunard; I know no more than any other member of the Phoenix Society. I am not of the inner circle; only this can I say, that there are few of the

26 April [Postmark 1923]   *121 Ebury Street*

Dearest Maud,

Your letter went to Howard, who I suppose will send
it on to you. It was to tell you that I go to Paris tomorrow,
Friday, for a month. I heard an opera last night, *The
Immortal Hour*, and it is a pity that the composer's craft is
not more highly developed, for he was inspired in the last
act—a small inspiration if you will, but still an inspiration,
and my watchword is always—hats off to an inspiration
however small. The choral writing seemed to me the
weakest part of the opera, which is moving despite his
weaknesses.[1]

Always affectionately yours George Moore

Sunday [Postmark 18 June 1923]   *121 Ebury Street*

My dear Maud,

Nancy sent a messenger with a letter asking me to tea
this afternoon and I told her messenger that I would be
with you between four and five, but I fell into a sickness
from which I could not rouse myself (a bilious attack I

Phoenix who have not heard it reported that her influence counted
for much in getting the money that saved the Old Vic. Among
much that is uncertain it seems certain that without Lady Cunard
we should not have had a London opera season in 1921. Does our
last opera season go back to 1920? I do not know. My admiration
for this warm-hearted, courageous woman compels me to praise
her whenever her name is mentioned, and to recall to the remem-
brance of everybody that she is the one woman in London society
whose thought for art extends beyond the narrow range of
ordering a portrait to be painted and setting on foot an intrigue for
the hanging of it in the National Gallery.

[1] *The Immortal Hour*, by Rutland Boughton, with libretto by the
composer based on works by "Fiona Macleod", was first produced
at Glastonbury in 1914. Between 1922 and 1924 it had a long run at
the Regent Theatre in London.

think) and I hope you will forgive me for not keeping my appointment.

I have to thank you for your invitation to your ball which I hear was delightful.

Always yours George Moore

20 June [Postmark 1923]   *121 Ebury Street*

Dearest Maud,

How is it I never hear from you? You are not angry with me again, and if you are write to me, for I have not the least idea of what it may be about. And my play? You have not had time to look into it. And *Gabrielle*? Are you coming to the first performance? It will be beautifully played: I have got the right people.

Always yours George Moore

Sunday [Postmark 2 July 1923]

Dearest Maud,

The Coming of Gabrielle is announced for the 12th.[1] Athene Seyler is wonderful, a better actress certainly than Réjane. It will be well to see the play from the beginning and it would be a great pleasure to me if you would come here. Is half an hour too much to ask? . . . I hope you liked the article in the *Fortnightly*.[2] Perhaps you have not seen it.

Always yours George Moore

[1] Three performances of *The Coming of Gabrielle* were given at the St James's Theatre in July 1923 (see note, p. 33).

[2] The dialogue between G.M. and Granville-Barker which appeared in the *Fortnightly Review* for July 1923 was afterwards incorporated in *Conversations in Ebury Street* (1924). See note, p. 124.

Monday night [*? August 1923*]   *121 Ebury Street*

My dear Maud,

It surprised and gladdened me to recognise your handwriting on an envelope addressed to me. I thought you would never write to me again. But why you invite me to come to see you instead of coming here puzzles me, and I ask myself to what idle tale you have given your credulous ear. For you are, do you know it? strangely credulous.

Would it suit your convenience for me to call tomorrow, Tuesday, or will you fix a day and hour when your house will not be overrun?

With the same affection George Moore

Sunday [*Postmark 12 November 1923*]   *121 Ebury Street*

Dearest Maud,

Steer spoke last night of a picture on show at Chapman's, gilder-framemaker, 241 King's Road, Chelsea, and from what he said I think it might suit you. A Venetian picture he said it was, of the time of Canaletto—not so good but a genuine picture that would furnish a house agreeably. Go to see it tomorrow, for the price is but £20 and from what Steer said I do not think it will remain long unsold. I cannot go with you tomorrow but any other day of the week I am at your service. You might ask them to reserve it till Tuesday.

Always affectionately yours George Moore

Sunday [*?February 1924*]   *121 Ebury Street*

There are two women in my life, Héloïse and Maud. Héloïse is with me by night and day; but Maud has passed into a fiercer light than any that beats upon a throne, and my life floats on 'twixt meditations on Héloïse and

127

memories of Maud. Dearest, when your ball is over you must come to the National Gallery to see there your (serious) rival's great picture.

The discoverer of Maud and Manet[1]

Sunday [? *1924*]   *Ritz Hotel*
My dear Maud,   *London*

You make engagements as you make curl-papers, and you drop them like curl-papers, and then you make more if you please[2]. . . Opposite me is a handsome dark woman. She has just bowed to me and I am without any faintest idea who she is. A friend of yours probably. And now about Thursday. I will dine with you and go to the theatre with you. But you will throw me away once more like a curl-paper. Why don't you come to Ebury Street and eat my simple fare?

Ever yours George Moore

[1] The National Gallery acquired its first two Manets (*La Musique aux Tuileries* and *Portrait of Eva Gonzales*) in 1917 under the bequest of Sir Hugh Lane. Two further works of minor importance were acquired in 1918, and in 1924 the *Serveuse de Bocks*, which must be the picture referred to here, though in fact it was acquired for the Tate Gallery, and first exhibited there in February. At this time G.M. was busy revising *Héloïse and Abélard* for the Uniform Edition of 1925.

[2] Cf. Congreve's *The Way of the World*, act ii, sc. iv:
Witwoud. Pray, Madam, do you pin up your Hair with all your Letters; I find I must keep Copies.
Millamant. Only with those in Verse, Mr Witwoud. I never pin up my Hair with Prose. . . . Lord, what is a Lover, that it can give? Why one makes Lovers as fast as one pleases, and they die as soon as one pleases: and then if one pleases one makes more.
Nigel Playfair's production of the play, with Edith Evans in the part of Millamant, opened at the Lyric Hammersmith on 7 February 1924 and drew the town for 158 performances. I have tentatively dated this letter accordingly.

Dearest Maud,

I had a copy of *Daphnis and Chloe* for you, but you have bought one and I am sorry you did.[1] I cannot spell the name of the street Nancy lives in. Will you send it to me so that I may send her a copy. I hope to see you soon—to see you is my only pleasure now and Rarely Rarely comest thou, spirit of delight.

As ever George Moore

Monday night   *121 Ebury Street*
[Postmark 10 February 1925]

Dearest Maud,

I cannot go to bed without writing to thank you for a delightful evening. Beecham's rendering of the *Siegfried Idyll* brought back all the old enchantment. I followed it bar by bar, and the Mozart that came before was exquisitely rendered, and the Mozart that followed Lalo's mechanisms rose phrase after phrase inspired always.[2] I shall go to the next symphony concert and hope to see you there.

Always affectionately yours George Moore

P.S. Heinemann is publishing an edition de luxe of *Hail and Farewell*—a thoroughly revised text. It would look well in your new house, and your acceptance of the two volumes will greatly please G.M.

[1] *The Pastoral Loves of Daphnis and Chloe*, done into English by George Moore, was published in a limited edition in December 1924.

[2] On 9 February 1925 at the Queen's Hall Sir Thomas Beecham conducted the London Symphony Orchestra in a concert which included Lalo's *Symphonie Espagnole* and Delius's *Paris*.

Thursday night [*?12 February 1925*]   [*121 Ebury Street*]

Dearest Maud,

I have not been feeling very well for some days past. Overwork I think and the weather are responsible. Certainly I am not my natural self, and that is perhaps why I could not stay to hear the last piece: *Paris*. I hope I shall see you next week. Lord Ivor Churchill called to see my pictures and I found him a most interesting young man and hope to see him again.[1] Should you be passing my way I hope you will come in. Your splendid health and spontaneity will encourage me to get well.

As ever yours, dearest and best friend a man ever had,

George Moore

Wednesday [*?1925*]   *121 Ebury Street*

My dear Maud,

Thank you for asking me to luncheon but the middle of the day is always devoted to literature; I must hold by my rule never to lunch, at home or abroad. I enjoyed the opera last night and admired the evenness of the playing. I think the conductor did very well indeed and feel sure that many people (not you) think that a man interprets the music if he conducts himself like a dancing Jenny. Richter didn't, but he was old fashioned, I believe.

Always yours George Moore

19 April [*1925*]   *121 Ebury Street*

Dearest Maud,

I enclose a letter which I hope you will send on to Nancy, for it is about her poem and she will be glad to

[1] Lord Ivor Spencer-Churchill (1898–1956), younger son of the ninth Duke of Marlborough, patron of art and artists.

hear that I find much good in it.[1] I shall be in Paris on the 15 or 20 of May; I cannot leave London any sooner. You will not have returned to London I hope. Do let me know your movements.

Always affectionately yours George Moore

Sunday night [*1925*]

Dearest Maud,

This is a note to thank you—I cannot go to bed without thanking you for the many hours we spent together sitting for our portraits.[2] The only hours that have any pleasure in them are those that I spend with you; the rest of my life, the hours that I spend writing, are drugged hours—work keeps me from thinking and I am thankful that I have my work.

Dearest and best of women, life would be a dreary thing without you. Come to see me soon.

Always yours George Moore

[*?8 May 1925*]   [*121 Ebury Street*]

Dearest Maud,

On looking into my manuscript I find that I have to write it all over again, a friend Moncrieff is waiting for these prefatory pages and the publishing season is going by.[3] I cannot do else than finish it, and to finish it I must stay at home tomorrow, Saturday. I am sorry. Like many

---

[1] *Parallax* by Nancy Cunard (1925).

[2] This seems likely to refer to the picture by Sir John Lavery reproduced opposite. It is dated 1925 on the back.

[3] G.M.'s Prefatory Letter to *The Letters of Abélard and Héloïse, now first translated from the Latin by C. K. Scott Moncrieff*, is dated 14 May 1925, though the next letter shows that he was still working on it in June. The book was not published till October.

other things it cannot be helped. Tell Lady Juliet that I am sorry and take me to see Princess Nicholas next week any day you like.

As ever George Moore

I am reading an exquisite book, *La Leçon d'Amour dans un Parc*.[1] You shall have it. Ask Lady Juliet if she has read it.

[*June 1925*]   [*121 Ebury Street*]

Dearest Maud,

Your letter arrived at 7 o'clock this evening, delayed possibly by the heat. Mabel tells me you posted it in the morning. I am sorry it did not arrive earlier, for a visit from you would have made me forget the heat and saved me from a publisher's office, whither I had to go to apologise for not being able to finish a prefatory letter for Moncrieff's translation of the letters of Abélard and Héloïse. I shall rise early at seven o'clock in the hope I may be able to write then. I am sending a bit of news that will down the critic, a sledgehammer blow. Bernard Shaw admires *The Cherry Orchard* more than any modern play and he denounced the stupidity of the first audiences that heard it.[2] Mr Macdonald Hastings may have been

---

[1] By René Boylesve (1867–1926), published in 1902.

[2] J. B. Fagan's production of Tchekov's play opened at the Lyric Theatre, Hammersmith, on 25 May 1925. Next day Basil Macdonald Hastings (1881–1928) dismissed it in the *Daily Express* as "this silly, tiresome, boring comedy . . . which has no conceivable relation with either drama or literature". On 4 June the *Express* printed this letter:

Sir, Twelve years ago Mr George Moore told me that *The Cherry Orchard* was the most perfect work of art which the modern theatre had produced.

The other night, at the Lyric Theatre, Hammersmith, I realised

one of the hissers. Be this as it may, he will be at his wits' end for an answer. He will be sprawling in the ring whilst Fagan shouts 'Shaw's words in writing to Mr George Moore were "an exquisite play", do you hear, an exquisite play.' He may add that the genius of Tchekov brought Shaw and Moore into agreement for the first and last time.

Yours G.M.

[*Postmark 17 August 1925*] *121 Ebury Street*

Dearest Maud,

It is pleasant to hear that I am not forgotten, but even if I were my feelings would not change, for as the years go by all but you vanish from me; the world is beginning to hold nothing else. Of course there is Nancy; to separate you from your daughter would be impossible. And this recessional mood, with me always of late years, is very much with me today, for I have finished *Ulick and Soracha* and the prospect of writing other books does [not] smile upon me. The future is sad and grey with no light in it but one. I am wondering now how I shall end my days. Sometimes I stand in front of shops that display fishing tackle and remember the flies I used to tie when I fished Lough Carra, and sometimes I think of a garden

---

that the haunting beauty and life-sense of this masterpiece can only be fully appreciated by those who have seen it on the stage.

I am moved to write out of pity for your numerous readers who, having read the divergent view of your dramatic critic, may be deprived of the greatest artistic enjoyment which the theatre can afford. Maud Cunard

On 10 June Macdonald Hastings replied in a long article entitled "Why *The Cherry Orchard* is a Bad Play". It consisted, he said, of "fatuous people talking drivel".

with a lilac avenue in bloom in May, and tall sunflowers over against a pretty paling in the autumn. I am thinking too of what you told me, that we may avoid income tax by living six months of the year in France; an excellent idea, for if I lived in France I should have to learn French. Greek too would suit me and there is no reason why Greek studies should not be continued in France. So perhaps the future is not so grey after all; and perhaps this break in the clouds may be attributed to the fact that I am addressing you. We shall meet, unless you rearrange your plans, in Paris in September or October. I am for the moment free from *Ulick and Soracha* and am without inclination to begin a volume of short tales, so let me know when you propose to leave Venice. It would be a catastrophe if you were to return to London the day that I cross to France. That occurred once and must not occur again. The day is exquisite here, a day betwixt summer and autumn, and it seems to me that I cannot do better than to let my pen run on, but into what gossip, narrative or criticism is my pen to run? My old friend Gosse has just published a beautiful article on Blake in the *Sunday Times*. Like another he writes well when he writes about what interests him, and the nearer the subject is to him the better he writes about it.[1] If that be the law that is over us, my letters to you should be among my best. Should be, only should be, for I am different from Gosse and often wonder how it is that I write best when the subject is far from my actual life. In *Ulick and Soracha* there is a servant Tadhg O Dorachy, a harper, and he is, if I am not mistaken, a serious rival to Esther Waters. Tadhg is the correct Irish spelling, but I am afraid the letters do not

[1] This article, entitled "Blake", appeared in the *Sunday Times* of 16 August 1925. It was a review of *The Writings of William Blake* (3 vols), edited by Geoffrey Keynes and published in a limited edition by the Nonesuch Press.

give the correct pronunciation—I doubt if they give any
pronunciation. This rhyme may help you:

> *Je suis O Dorachy, harpiste, prénom Tadhg;*
> *Ma harpe sur le dos je marche sans fatigue.*

This rhyme reminds me of another which I must have
sent to you:

> *Pourquoi vous plaignez-vous des ans, belle marquise?*
> *Une rose d'automne est plus qu'une autre exquise.*

The second line of this distich is famous, the first less so,
for it is mine.[1]

I enclose Gosse's article; it may interest you to read.
And now I must write to tell Gosse that I sat like one
enchanted whilst reading it. Have you seen Lord Berners?
He lent me a volume of Mérimée's dramatic writings and
I am unable to imagine anybody choosing to write music
for the comedy *Du Saint-Sacrement*.[2] It is altogether
without emotion, and I always understood that emotion
is the soul of music, not only of music but of all the arts.
One lives even if one does not learn.

Always affectionately yours George Moore

8 October [Postmark 1925]   *121 Ebury Street*

Dearest Maud,

I am here still scribbling, beginning and completing
stories, and casting sheep's eyes at Paris for you are there.

[1] On 21 November 1922 G.M. quoted the second line in a letter
to Dujardin, commenting: "Who wrote this pretty line? Malherbe,
I think?" On 16 December he followed this by a postcard: "I don't
like the single verse: add, therefore: *Pourquoi vous plaignez-vous des
ans, chère marquise?*" The second line comes from Book iv of *Les
Tragiques* (1616) by Théodore Agrippa d'Aubigné (1552–1630).

[2] Lord Berners's opera *Le Carrosse du Saint-Sacrement*, based on
Mérimée's comedy, had been performed in Paris on 24 April 1924.

If I could catch you in the humour for such poor society as my soul affords I'd pack my trunk. Why are you not at the Ritz? Is Paris very full? If I go I'll write a week ahead. The Continental will find a room for me.

As ever, dearest friend, yours George Moore

17 October 1925   *121 Ebury Street*

Dearest Maud,

I received your postcard this morning and was very glad to get it, and what you say about, perhaps, having to come back to England at once reminds me of something I have longed for years to possess—a pretty *chocolatière* with accessories: salver (*plateau*), two cups and saucers, milk jug and sugar basin. If you will avoid fashionable shops and seek the *chocolatière* in the Quartier Latin, you will probably get a pretty one, Eighteenth-Century, Directoire or *thereabouts* (not Empire). You will get one for 1200 francs or 1500. I saw a pretty one in Fontainebleau quite genuine for that price. I will send you the money and hope you will not return the cheque. The service I saw in Fontainebleau was chocolate-coloured but if the decoration be pretty, one colour is as good as another. Sèvres is too expensive and I care little for it. However one must take things as they come and I have waited too long already. But do not exceed the price named.

Always affectionately George Moore

17 October [Postmark 1925]   *121 Ebury Street*
Five o'clock

Dearest Maud,

I wrote to you today at noon about a chocolate pot, and this letter should arrive at the same time as the letter I am writing at four in the evening in answer to your telegram. I can come to Paris next week not earlier than Thursday. If you remain in Paris till the 1st of November, I'll write to the Continental to engage a room. Only at the Continental is the kind of room known in which I can sleep: because I am the oldest customer (I go back to the day the hotel opened) the Continental will make every effort to oblige me. But let me know as soon as you can.

Always affectionately yours George Moore

I dined last night at Lady Lavery's. I sat next Lady Curzon who was in Venice with you and we talked of you through several courses.

Sunday [Postmark 26 October 1925]   *121 Ebury Street*

Dearest Maud,

Sometimes the expected happens, and your insistence that I must accept the *chocolatière* as a present was not unforeseen. I dare not commit myself to words on the subject lest I should bring a frown into your dear face. I hope to be in Paris on the fifth or sixth of November. If you cross before that date let me know, for I should not like—I mean that it would grieve me—to leave London on the day you arrive. That happened once and it must not happen again. I have finished *Ulick and Soracha* and to my satisfaction, but the writing of this last long book has tired me more than you can imagine and more than any words can tell. I need change and am going to Paris in search of change, but what I need more than change is you. I must see you here or in Paris. It doesn't matter which. Do write and save me from a misadventure that will spoil my rest if it should fall out that we should not meet each other next week.

Always affectionately yours G.M.

137

27 October 1925   *121 Ebury Street*

Dearest Maud,

I am crossing tomorrow, Wednesday. I must get a change of air, am feeling run down and hope the French air, French food and the French language will resuscitate the old Adam in me still.

Always affectionately yours George Moore

[? 28–31 October 1925]   *Hotel Continental*
                                                            Paris

Dearest Maud,

The evening seemed empty without you. Will you dine with me on Tuesday and we will go to any place of amusement that takes your fancy. Music suits me best but it will be a pleasure to be with you whatever the art may be.

Always affectionately yours George Moore

Is the lunch for Wednesday week *certain* and *sure?* As soon as the arrangements are made I will begin to write my little speech which I hope will please you, dear; nobody else could persuade me, but having been persuaded I shall be disappointed if it does not come to pass.

As ever, dearest friend, George Moore

Sunday [*1 November 1925*]   *Hotel Continental*
                                                            Paris

Dearest Maud,

I waited for you but I suppose you could not get here after the Fight.[1] Do ask for me always, for it may be that I have gone to my room. I am often tired, I don't know

[1] On 31 October 1925 in Paris, Francis Charles won the light-heavyweight championship of France, knocking out Bonnel, the holder, in the sixth round.

138

why—the weather perhaps. Tomorrow I have a dinner engagement, otherwise I am free. I enjoyed the music, hearing it and thinking about it.

Always affectionately yours George Moore

P.S. What an extraordinarily charming man!—our host at breakfast. I liked [him] more than anybody I have seen for some time.

[Postmark 5 November 1925]   Hotel Continental
                                                      Paris

Dearest Maud,
I have bad news for you. I have been trying all day to write a speech. I have tried in French and in English and have failed equally in both languages. I cannot find anything suitable to say, that is the root of the difficulty. I am writing to Monsieur Henry Soulie in despair, begging him to undertake to tell the company that I am sensible and grateful to everybody but am unable to speak even a few words of thanks—he must speak my thanks for me. There is no going back on this. I have put you in a hole and myself in a deeper one. A man that has refused to speak in public for forty years knows the truth.

Always affectionately yours George Moore

Will you write to Monsieur Henry Soulie and smooth away the difficulty?

[November 1925]   Hotel Continental
                                                      Paris

Dearest Maud,
I enclose the little speech I wrote because you wished it. I loved you in the beginning and shall love you to the end.

As ever George Moore

Monday night [November 1925]　　　　　*Hotel Continental*
　　　　　　　　　　　　　　　　　　　　　　　Paris

Dearest Maud,

　I have an appointment at 60 Avenue du Bois tomorrow
Tuesday at five o'clock which I cannot forgo, and afterwards I have an appointment with Lady Abdy at 59
Avenue Victor Hugo to sign some books. I cannot forgo
this appointment either, and you would not like me to I
know, so what is to be done? After the luncheon at the
Embassy I shall return here and at three o'clock I shall be
here and shall wait in the hope of seeing you till 4.30.
With the same affection and gratitude George Moore

[November 1925]　　　　　　　　　　*Hotel Continental*
　　　　　　　　　　　　　　　　　　　　　　　Paris

Dearest Maud,

　I return to London dreaming of my *été de la St Martin*—
my Indian summer, and the day long ago when I saw you
in a grey shot-silk gown.

　　　　　　　　　　　　Always yours George Moore

9 December [1925]　　　　　　　　　　*121 Ebury Street*

Dearest Maud,

　I am glad you like the dedication.[1] Balzac never wrote
well except in the dedications of his books, and as I do

---

[1] The dedication of *Ulick and Soracha* runs:

Dear Lady of my thoughts, dear Lady Cunard, time turns all
things into analogues and symbols, and in the course of the years I
have come to think of you as an evening fountain under em-
bosoming trees. The fountain murmurs, sings, exults; it welcomes
every coming minute; and when the dusk deepens in the garden
and the gallants enfold their ladies in scarves and veils and the
rout disperses, the fountain sings alone the sorrows of the water-
lilies to the moon.　George Moore

not want to fall too far behind him I am grateful to you for your assistance. It will convenience me if you will let me know if it will suit you to dine here with me and Tonks next Wednesday. Tonks cannot manage Friday. The Slade is 'hopping' on Friday evening.

Always affectionately yours George Moore

I will call for you at the Ritz at 1.45 on Saturday and hope to find you on the steps.

17 December 1925   *121 Ebury Street*

Dearest Maud,

I enclose an article from the *Spectator* which seems to prelude a new departure in my literary history.[1] You will meet Tonks on Saturday night, acknowledged to be one of the most agreeable and winning and sympathetic men in London.[2] By the way, what is Evan Charteris's[3] number in Mount Street, and shall I call for you or meet you there?

Always affectionately yours George Moore

Sunday night [*?20 December 1925*]

You were enchanting last night at dinner, so alert, so witty, so enveigling—never were you brighter or more wonderful. More like a fountain. I thought of you for a

[1] An unsigned review of the Uniform Edition of *Héloïse and Abélard* had appeared in the *Spectator* of December 5. Its glowing praise and insistence on G.M.'s superiority over Thomas Hardy must have particularly delighted him.

[2] G.M. must have forgotten that long ago Tonks had stayed with Lady Cunard at Nevill Holt. See p. 78.

[3] The Hon. Sir Evan Charteris, K.C. (1864–1940), sixth son of the tenth Earl of Wemyss, barrister, chairman of the Tate Gallery, biographer of Edmund Gosse and J. S. Sargent.

long while afterwards and I am thankful you did not tell the story of the cat. Had you done so it would have appeared as part of my conversation or yours in the *Daily Express* and the subject would have been lost to me. You promised you would not tell it and you kept your word. The rug is rich and it lights up the room.

Affectionately yours George Moore

Saturday night [*?2 January 1926*]

Dearest Maud,

I was needless to say glad to get your letter written from Switzerland and I would have answered it at once if I had not been detained by the chapters I am adding to *Ulick and Soracha*. The fact is that I found myself again in a blind alley and on the 31st of December was about to throw up the sponge and withdraw the book, paying the publishers of course for the composition. But a night of insomnia revealed the long-sought-for secret, and on the 1st of January I was a new Narcissus delighted like my progenitor with myself—my spiritual self. I hope to finish this terrible book during the coming week. But why do you seek new doctors? You always seem to be in the best of health; your looks proclaim your health. Forgive my solicitude. Perhaps I should have allowed your discovery to pass without comment. I am going to spend this evening with Tonks, whom I have not seen for quite a time. Nancy called here and we had a long talk and walked to Hyde Park Corner together, and would have walked farther if the rain hadn't come on. The subject of our conversation was her prose story. I told her the lines I wrote about you and she seemed to like them. By the way, I am embarrassed to find a title: what do you think of *An Appreciation*? Or do you think that *Evocation* would

142

be a better title? The Laureate whom I consulted sent me a Latin word which I cannot decipher alas.[1]

Always affectionately yours George Moore

Do come and see me the day you return, to see me and "your" rug. But I am your rug.

7 January 1926   121 Ebury Street

Dearest Maud,

I enclose the letters I received from you this morning, one from Jones[2] and one from Balfour. For the OM in its relation to me I do not care twopence, but in its relation to you I care a great deal, for it reminds me; I need no reminding, for your kindness and sweetness of heart are never long out of my thoughts; all the same it is pleasant to be reminded that I was permitted to know intimately a beautiful soul. You brought a beautiful soul into the world, and when you die the world will have lost something of more worth to me than any book or picture. I cannot write more today: I am tired, for every day I strive with the narrative of *Ulick and Soracha*. The book is in type but I have had to write the beginning over again,

[1] G.M. was clearly seeking a title for his dedication of *Ulick and Soracha* to Lady Cunard. On 21 December 1925 he wrote to the Poet Laureate, Robert Bridges: "The usual formula, Epistle Dedicatory, is too stiff and heavy for the enclosed lines, and it is impertinent to ask you to suggest a Latin title."

[2] This name is almost indecipherable, but may refer to Tom Jones, then Secretary to the Cabinet. Clearly Lady Cunard tried for some time to persuade the authorities to award G.M. the Order of Merit. On 4 September 1926 Arnold Bennett noted in his journal: "Lady C . . . wanted me to exert myself to get the O.M. for George Moore. She said that Balfour was favourable but would never actually do anything to help anyone." G.M. never received this or any other honour.

adding two new chapters, and these I write in feverish anxiety lest I should fail again.

Dearest woman, always yours George Moore

19 January [Postmark 1926]   *121 Ebury Street*

Dearest Maud,

I have left you a long time without a letter, but this was not negligence but necessity. *Ulick and Soracha* is in type but not yet finished and I spend five or six hours every day at it and shall have to go on in the same way for another fortnight. I miss you. There is nobody to take me to concerts and I have no pleasure now except the pleasure that I get out of good music and your conversation which is always good.

Always affectionately yours George Moore

5 February [Postmark 1926]   *121 Ebury Street*

Dearest Maud,

I waited a long time for the letter I received this morning and for a day without thought for that horrid book *Ulick and Soracha*. It went wrong again and I was frightened that I would not be able to finish it and might have to withdraw the book. You can imagine my mental trouble and will forgive me for not having written sooner. Will you let me know when you return to Paris, for I can promise you to be there to meet you if your return be not delayed beyond the 16th. I am lunching with Lord Ivor on Tuesday and will write you a letter about the people I meet.

Always affectionately yours, dearest Maud,

George Moore

Dearest Maud,

I was very sorry not to have been able to drive with you to Grosvenor Square. But I have received documents relative to the sums of money I am to get from the Free State for the burning of my house,[1] and these I have neglected to attend to day after day, and I had arranged with my secretary to dictate suitable answers to certain questions, and I did not dare to again postpone this business. To have missed another post would have caused inconvenience and perhaps prejudiced my case. As it was I arrived home none too soon, at four o'clock. I congratulate you on your new acquisitions: the Russell is in my taste.

I am not yet convinced that anybody has thought of conferring on me the Order of Merit; I cannot rid myself of the belief that you are dreaming, but if you are not dreaming and the order should be offered to me I should be loath to write a refusal of it; to do so would be an unseemly act, and the rather since you are the promoter of the idea.

Dearest Maud, I am yours always George Moore

23 March [*Postmark 1926*]   *121 Ebury Street*

Dearest Maud,

I have thought of you every day, sitting in my lonely house listening for the postman, and now I have to wait till Saturday before seeing you and showing you your portrait.

Always affectionately yours George Moore

[1] G.M.'s old home, Moore Hall in County Mayo, had been burnt down by Republicans in 1923.

25 June [*1926*] [*121 Ebury Street*]

Dearest Maud,

I received this morning an advance copy of *Ulick and Soracha*. The book will not be published till the twenty-eighth, but I cannot wait till then to show you the inscription and the fountain.[1] Would you like me to come to luncheon tomorrow or would you like me to meet you at the Ritz after luncheon at 3.30? Or would Sunday suit you better? Will you send me word?

Always affectionately yours George Moore

12 August 1926 *121 Ebury Street*

Dearest Maud,

I don't feel as if I were going to write any more big stories: I may, but I can't forget that I have been writing without interruption for forty years, and if I cease to write my income will be diminished till I shall hardly be able to live in Ebury Street. Wherefore I am thinking, asking myself, if it would not be wise to sell five valuable pictures and invest the money in Liberty Bonds, the best security in the world. By will you will inherit the money these pictures will fetch, the pictures should fetch something between fifteen and twenty thousand pounds. Now what do you think of this? The sentimental side will be amply satisfied by the books and the other pictures. If you think well of this you might be able to arrange the matter with Sir Joseph.[2] Don't forget that

[1] *Ulick and Soracha* was published in a limited edition by the None-such Press on 28 June 1926. Opposite the dedication (see note, p. 140) was printed a copper-plate engraving of a fountain by Stephen Gooden.

[2] Sir Joseph (later Lord) Duveen (1869–1939), the art dealer. G.M. never, in fact, sold any of his pictures.

the pictures have acquired a certain extra value because they belonged to me, Manet's prophet for many years. Moreover I am often nervous lest the pictures should be stolen one night—the burning of Moore Hall has made me nervous.

I am glad to hear you are feeling better. The London season tried your health and nerves, you were suffering from nerves the night you dined at Leverton Harris's.[1]

With undying love I am as ever yours George Moore

[? *August 1926*]   *121 Ebury Street*

Dearest Maud,

As you are to inherit all my literature you will need a literary adviser—one who is intimately acquainted with my ideas and who is possessed of enough knowledge of literature and sense of literature to point out and to suggest, to write a preface. Ernest Longworth[2] can do much more; he is writing a dramatic version of *Héloïse and Abélard*[3] and I should like you to meet him. He is a very old friend of mine and I am nearly sure you will like him. Will you dine here to meet him before you leave London? You were a society talker during dinner at the Harris's, but the moment we got into the street you became the sweet kind woman that I have always loved for her intellect and her beauty—for herself and nothing but herself—a strain of lovely music that has run through my life.

Always yours, dearest Maud, George Moore

[1] The Rt Hon. Frederick Leverton Harris, M.P. (1864–1926).

[2] An Irish barrister friend of G.M.'s who combined legal knowledge with literary taste and helped G.M. a great deal with the proofs of his books. Longworth was at one time secretary to Sir Horace Plunkett.

[3] This was never published or produced, and may not even have been finished. See p. 151.

Dearest Maud,

The pictures that I would sell are the two Manets, the two Morisots, the Monet and a Degas pastel. These are valuable pictures and will become more and more valuable. If Sir Joseph will buy I will sell (with your permission), invest the money and leave it to you. But, dearest Maud, all you tell me about your health terrifies me. You have been to twenty doctors and their prescriptions have not cured you. But I know what will cure if you will try it, and if you don't you will lose your health permanently. Rest is what you need. You have excellent health really but put too great a strain upon it. The London season that you have just come out [of] and which you are going to find again in Venice will prove your undoing if you cannot be persuaded to abjure. I shuddered when I read the words "I am going to Venice," for what you need is a long rest cure in a home, and when you have endured it for about two months you will leave it to change your life, to seek and find contentment in the country. To mend your excellent constitution which you have tried severely you must do all this; the doctors can't help you, you must help yourself. I am speaking in my own interest as much as in yours, for if you were to go I cannot imagine—I dare not try to imagine—the end of my own life. I should die of grief to put it plainly, of a deadly melancholy that nothing could cure or stay. One word more, in Venice you will find the turmoil that has unnerved you. Put yourself in a doctor's orders at once and when you are well live reasonably. Be assured of this: *there is no other way.*

Always affectionately G.M.

30 September [1926]   *121 Ebury Street*

Dearest Maud,

Your lover of other days is mystified and chagrined today. At the end of a graceful and charming letter came a new signature "Maud Emerald (a new name)."[1] I took your letter to Tonks and his words were "Is she married?" I answered "I can put no other meaning on it". After considering carefully he said he did not know of anybody called Emerald, and after searching the telephone book he declared the name to be a mere whimsy, no more serious than a new plume in a hat. But I don't feel sure, far from it, that he is right and I beg you to send me a telegram. A yes or a no will be enough. You cannot fail to understand that it is unfair to leave a man who has loved you dearly for more than thirty years in doubt.

As ever George Moore

[*Telegram*]

1 October 1926   *London*

Lady Cunard, Beau Rivage Palace, Ouchy, Lausanne

WHO IS EMERALD ARE YOU MARRIED? G.M.[2]

[1] Lady Cunard had decided that she would discard the name Maud in favour of Emerald, by which she was known for the rest of her life.

[2] This same day G.M. wrote to Edmund Gosse: "I telegraphed . . . and at the end of the day the news came: 'Emerald is not a man, but the jewels I wear are emeralds and they have gained me a nickname, The Emerald Queen.' Rossetti says in a little poem ["Autumn Song"] that the greatest happiness is the passing of pain, and yesterday I felt he was right." On 2 October 1926 Sir Joseph Duveen wrote to Lady Cunard from the S.S. *Berengaria*:

"Since my last letter to you I have again seen Mr George Moore, and must relate to you an extraordinary incident. He was awaiting

16 November [?1926][1]   *Central Hotel*
Dearest Maud,   *Limoges*
   On my way back to Paris from the Pyrenees I write to
tell you that I found the thorpe or town needed to locate

---

me in the dining room, and I thought he looked rather perturbed as
I approached him. He at once gave me a letter to read, a four-page
one, and after perusing it I remarked that I did not see anything in
it to cause undue excitement—that it was just a very sweet and charming letter from a friend; and I asked him why it excited him so
much. "But can't you see how it is signed?" he asked. "Don't you
see it is signed 'Yours sincerely, Maud Emerald'? and then in brackets
below 'This is my new name'." I noticed on the table near him a
telephone book and two or three directories; and he then told me
that he had spent the morning pacing up and down the room like a
caged animal trying to find out who Mr Emerald was! and he could
find only one name! and he a paint manufacturer! Of course, he
thought you had married again and were now Mrs Emerald. After I
had recovered from my amusement I explained to him that your
friends often called you the Queen of the Emeralds, and that I myself
had often thought of you as such whenever I saw you wearing those
wonderful jewels in which you look so brilliant, which suit your
personality so well and of which you are so fond; and remembering
that, at the moment of signing your letter to him, you had spon-
taneously added the word "Emerald." He appeared greatly relieved,
but said he had been upset all day—he certainly looked quite ill, and
began to cry. I stayed with him an hour, reassuring him and putting
him at his ease, and told him that I would anyhow be writing to you
and must really relate the incident. I am sure you will be just as much
amused as I was. As I told you in my last letter, we have become very
friendly. He is one of the dearest souls I have ever met, and you are
perfectly right about his charming character. I told him I wanted to
take him to America with me some day."

[1] All efforts to date this letter have failed. No trace can be found of
G.M.'s visit to the Pyrenees or of the story in question. It may have
been intended for the volume called *In Minor Keys* (see note, p. 156).
That possibility, and the fact that Nancy Cunard was in Paris only
from 1921 to early 1927, suggests 1926 as a possible year. Moreover,
on 4 November 1926 G.M. wrote to A. J. A. Symons: "I am tele-
graphing to Paris for a room and hope to start at the end of the week,
but I shall not be away for more than a month at most."

the story I have in mind, but were I to begin a description of the loveliness of the river and the miraculous mountains, and the soft voluptuous sunshine and the yellow and orange foliage, I should miss my train. Of my good fortune you shall hear when you come to luncheon in December, for I shall delay a few days in Paris, not many, to see some publishers. Nancy dined with me and we spent a long evening together and we talked on many subjects. You were the principal subject, naturally; and if she did not feel that I would begin my life again for your sake she lacks perception. Yet nothing precise was said and I shall see her again before I see you.

With love and affection George Moore

Monday night 121 *Ebury Street*
[*Postmark 14 December 1926*]

Dearest Maud,

Your letter inviting me to meet you at 21 Park Lane and to go with you to the concert arrived here this morning delayed in the post, a thing that often happens at this season of the year. I hope to see you soon and to give you *Héloïse and Abélard* (play) to read. It is coming out very well. The first two acts were a puzzle but they have been unravelled, I think.[1]

Always affectionately yours George Moore

5 January [*Postmark 1927*] 121 *Ebury Street*

Dearest Maud,

When the telephone message was handed to me I took it to be a summons to come to your bedside, and my disappointment was great when I read that you were too

---

[1] See note, p. 147.

ill tonight to see anybody. I hope to have better news tomorrow and you will not delay to send for me I hope.

The same as ever George Moore

9 January [*1927*]   *121 Ebury Street*

Dearest Maud,

Yesterday I lunched with Evan Charteris and after lunch I walked to Grosvenor [Square] to learn that I had missed you by a couple of hours. You can imagine my dismay better than I can describe it. Worse still [is] the fact that you will not return to London till April. I can't help thinking that it was cruel of you to go away without seeing me.

The same as ever George Moore

[*Typewritten except for first and last lines*]

14 January 1927   *121 Ebury Street*

Dearest Maud,

You will forgive me for writing through a secretary when I tell you that I am too enfeebled by a heavy cold to leave my armchair. I was, as I told you in my letter, disappointed at finding I had missed you by a couple of hours after leaving Evan Charteris, with whom I am dining on Tuesday if I am well enough. I am glad to hear that you are coming back in February and read with pleasure what the *Daily Mail* had to say about your scamper out of England in search of sunshine.

With love George Moore

Friday 21 January [*1927*]   *121 Ebury Street*

Dearest Maud,

My cold has turned out so bad a one that I have not been able to leave the house for the last ten days and my pitch is still my fireside. As soon as I am better the doctor proposes to send me away for change of air. Hence my silence. This note is to tell you that you will find in the *Revue des Deux Mondes* for January 15 (the last number) a long article about your book.[1]

Yours with love and affection George Moore

I had a long letter from Nancy who is leaving Paris.

3 March 1927   *121 Ebury Street*

Dearest Maud,

This letter is to tell you before I have the delight of seeing you that I long to see your face and to hear your voice. Since you left London I have worked hard, but work is not enough and I have felt constantly how much I need you and for good reason—you are the only real thing I have met in life, real to me. And better kill a man than deprive him of the woman he needs.

With much love George Moore

Sunday 20 March [1927]   *121 Ebury Street*

Dearest Maud,

Last Monday I consulted a specialist and he put me on a diet which he said I must follow if I wished to live a little longer. His words were "Your life is your own and it is up to you to save it." My health responded instantly to the diet and last night I enjoyed a night's rest, sleeping from midnight till seven. I tell you this for I wish you to understand it was not weariness of spirit that obliged me to leave your luncheon table last Sunday but physical pain. But do not be alarmed, I am already nearly well and

[1] The *Revue des Deux Mondes* of 15 January 1927 contained a twelve-page review by Louis Gillet of the American edition of *Ulick and Soracha*.

153

v

shall remain well if I refrain from sugar. The specialist told me to come to him again in a fortnight, which I shall do, and it will not surprise me if he tells me that I am in specialist language "sugar free." Tomorrow I am going to Bath for three days, returning on Thursday. A visit from you on Thursday or Friday will be a great pleasure to me, and the visit will remind me of the kind responsive heart in you.

I enclose a letter from Nancy, which I hope will please you. At the end of the month I shall go to Paris to sign the review copies of *The Brook Kerith*.[1]

Always affectionately yours George Moore

Friday night [?March-April 1927]　　　*121 Ebury Street*

Dearest Maud,

The severity of the dieting has wrecked my wits. I can but lie in an armchair and allow my thoughts to wander; and as my state will probably be no better tomorrow than it is today I think it will be better to postpone the projected visit of your friend at the embassy. I am sorry.

Very affectionately yours George Moore

Sunday night [Postmark 25 April 1927]

Dearest Maud,

You have not been to see me for a long time and our drive to Dulwich is postponed till June, for I am going to Paris for a month. My address in Paris will be the Continental and I will write to you if you will promise to write to me. I am sorry to miss seeing you before I go . . . What has kept you away? You have not been ill I hope.

The same as always George Moore

[1] A French translation, by Philippe Niel, entitled *Solitude du Kerith* was published in Paris in 1927.

Thursday 19 [Postmark May 1927]   *121 Ebury Street*

Dearest Maud,

I will come to luncheon on the 25th but is it fair for you to keep me away from you so long?

The same as ever George Moore

Monday night   *121 Ebury Street*
[Postmark 28 June 1927]

Dearest Maud,

I find that I cannot lunch with you on Wednesday and for the reason given in my letter. But I should like to see you and will call when it pleases you on Friday or Saturday. Shall I send you *The Making of an Immortal?*[1]

Affectionately yours George Moore

30 July [? 1927]   *121 Ebury Street*

Dearest Maud,

It was a blow to hear that you had called here and not found me at home. My parlourmaid spoke of the Ritz and I telephoned to the Ritz thinking you were dining there and might see me after dinner. It was then too late to go to Grosvenor Square and so the season has ended very blankly for me. If you go to Athens, go to Aulis and write to me about it and the long island of Euboea.

Your sad but always affectionate friend

George Moore

Wednesday [Postmark 24 August 1927]   *121 Ebury Street*

Dearest Maud,

I returned yesterday from Kent, whither I went in search

[1] G.M.'s comedy about Shakespeare, which was published in a limited edition in August 1927 and produced at the Arts Theatre on 1 April 1928.

of the beautiful health that has favoured me ever since I saw you in the shot-silk gown and before, but without recapturing much of what I have lost. Your postcard was my recompense, and my sorrow is that I cannot leave London till I finish my Greek story, my last story, for with the volume entitled *In Minor Keys*[1] I have accomplished my destiny—this sounds rather grander than it is, but we all have a destiny, and mine was clearly to love you always and to write narratives different from those written by my predecessors. I think I shall be in Paris in October and shall hope to see you there. I wish you would stay at the Continental, for then I should see you in the mornings, we could go out together, breakfast together. I know you are addicted to an audience—that is my misfortune. Alone you are enough for me, for you are yourself then and nothing but yourself. I hope you may try the Continental in October. I should like to go to Chantilly with you. You promised to return to Dulwich with me but circumstance robbed me of that pleasure; recompense me with Chantilly, for you are always associated with art in my thoughts, "dear lady of my thoughts, dear Lady Cunard."

Always affectionately yours George Moore

13 October [Postmark 1927]   *121 Ebury Street*

Dearest Maud,

I waited a long time for your handwriting but it came at last and I am waiting for your arrival in London. I am not

[1] On 14 October 1926 G.M. wrote to R. I. Best: "I am writing a volume of short tales to be called *In Minor Keys*." No such volume was ever published, but in May 1928 a contract was drawn up (though never signed) with the American publisher Crosby Gaige for the publication of a book of five short stories. Two stories (*At the Turn of the Road* and *Three Golden Fishes*), which appeared in the *Cosmopolitan* and *Nash's* in 1927 and 1928, may have been two of the five.

ill but my health is not quite the same as it was. I have to follow a strict diet and it is difficult to do this in Paris. Moreover I am bound hand and foot to *Aphrodite in Aulis*—the name of my Greek story, and dare not leave it till the whole text is on paper. As I shall not write any more "works" I am anxious that my last shall be among my best. I await your arrival. Give my love to Nancy. I would have written to her long ago if I had had her address. Perhaps you will send it or give it to me when you arrive.

As always George Moore

Monday night   *121 Ebury Street*
[*Postmark 25 October 1927*]

Dearest Maud,

I am looking forward to seeing you here, perchance, one afternoon this week. You will remember that you promised me a visit, feeling, no doubt, that I had earned one. And I am looking forward to going to the concert next Sunday. Would that I were sure of going there with you and not with a crowd of others. I have not heard a note of music since I saw you, nor seen any people except the people of my dream—*Aphrodite in Aulis*. I spend long evenings by myself lying almost at length in an armchair that has begotten many dreams. I look forward to the music and to you.

Always the same George Moore

Friday night   *121 Ebury Street*
[*Postmark 5 November 1927*]

Dearest Maud,

I was disappointed to hear you had called, and the disappointment fell heavy for I had spent most of the day writing *Aphrodite in Aulis*. It will give me much pleasure to dine with you on Monday 14th of November at eight forty-five. My head is heavy: I cannot write more at present.

With the same affection George Moore

Dearest Maud,

I am desperately sorry that I am engaged tomorrow, Friday, for to spend the evening with you and alone would be a real pleasure, and few real pleasures are left to me to enjoy. I lack courage to put off my guest; it would seem cruelly rude. Almost any other evening will suit me if you can spare an evening from your many occupations. In the telegram I sent you I mentioned Saturday and Sunday as being free days. On Monday Magee is coming up from Bournemouth and I promised to put him up for two nights. All the rest of the week is free. I work every day at *Aphrodite* and am beginning to spy rosy hopes on the horizon—hopes that will allow me to spend my last years in some sunny French village amid friends aestheticising the days away, my feet in the bluest and beautifullest of seas.[1] Of course you will be a constant visitor, dearest Maud. I never felt disappointment more keenly than I do today.   G.M.

Thursday [*Postmark 15 December 1927*]

Dearest Maud,

I was handed a packet of letters on the dark staircase and knew one of the letters came from you. If you knew the pleasure the sight of your face or handwriting gives me you would come to Ebury Street oftener and write

[1] See note, p. 87.

oftener, for you are instinctively kind. But this letter is not a complaint but a confession of how much you mean to me. Every year you mean more . . . I will come to luncheon on Saturday.

With ever increasing affection George Moore

Saturday 31 December [Postmark 1927]

Dearest Maud,

I am afraid I am not well enough to lunch with you tomorrow, Sunday, and shall spend the day instead by my fireside dozing and regretting the very poor letter that appeared in *The Times*.[1] Another thing. It is impossible for me to allow my name to appear among those who favour Sir Thomas Beecham's operatic schemes.[2] You know why. Please to select another name, and you will not blame me, for it would be unjust to do so.

With the same affection George Moore

Sunday [Postmark 9 January 1928]   *121 Ebury Street*

Dearest Maud,

Much as I would have liked to go to see you, I was persuaded not to risk the cold streets by the cold of the passages and staircase of my little house, cold enough to freeze a leg of mutton. I have spent the day sniffing eucalyptus, probably in vain. I hope you are well.

With much love and affection yours G.M.

[1] On 31 December 1927 *The Times* published a letter from G.M., replying to one on 29 December by A. A. Milne, who had attacked G.M. for publishing *The Making of an Immortal* at three guineas so that only the rich could buy it.

[2] A reference to the Imperial League of Opera, an ambitious scheme which failed in its full object owing to lack of subscriptions. It was, however, put into action in a limited form, and several operas were produced under its banner.

17 January [? 1928]   *121 Ebury Street*

Dearest Maud,

The hotel at Falmouth is excellent.[1] You can have a suite of rooms comprising bedroom, bathroom, sitting room and a room for your maid, *but* this is admitted to be an unfavourable moment to visit Falmouth. If you would care to spend two or three days in Falmouth and then go on to Mrs Eliot's[2] at St Germans you might get through a week without being bored beyond endurance. Let me know what you decide to do. If you decide against Falmouth I will write to Mrs Eliot and ask her if she will have me for four days or a week. I shall miss you terribly but St Moritz is too far, hours and hours in the train!

Always affectionately yours George Moore

19 January [? 1928]   *121 Ebury Street*

Dearest Maud,

I have received a letter from the Duchess of Rutland advising me to consult her doctor and I am about to post a letter thanking her for her kindness. But the last lines of her letter run as follows: "I have told Maud by letter re Metropole, Brighton." I hope she has not persuaded you from Falmouth. The Metropole Brighton sounds like Lady Sackville.   With much affection George Moore

4 February [1928]   *121 Ebury Street*

Dearest Maud,

I have read the *Times* article with attention and so far as I can see it contains nothing that can be answered effec-

---

[1] On 28 January 1928 G.M. wrote to John Eglinton: "I have just come from Falmouth, and a colder and more miserable village I never set foot in; we escaped as by a miracle with nothing worse than a couple of colds that will last till the Spring comes."

[2] The Hon Mrs Montague Eliot, now Countess of St Germans.

tively.[1] The writer says no more than that the Opera League cannot ask for a subsidy till it has come into being and shown what it can do. And it is hard to call the writer to account for having said so much. It would be my pleasure to obey your wishes but I fail to find an argument with which to dispute this point.

Affectionately George Moore

Tuesday [*Postmark 8 February 1928*]   *121 Ebury Street*

Dearest Maud,

You had only just left my house when I returned from Sir John Thompson [Walker]'s surgery at 96 Harley Street. I learnt from him that my case was not urgent and that he would give me two months to finish *Aphrodite in Aulis*. I begin the task of revision tomorrow. I have nothing more to tell you, for I am a little shaky this evening.

With all love and affection yours as ever

George Moore

1 March 1928   [*7 Portland Place*[2] *W.1.*]

My dear Maud,

This letter is to confirm all I said to you last night; that if I should die before you, most of my property will come to you. But the part of my property that will interest you will be my books, and to keep them in publication, properly advertised, and printed, you will need an editor, and I am sure that you will never find one who will be

---

[1] On 21 January 1928 *The Times* had published an anonymous article on the Imperial League of Opera, headed "Attitude towards Opera".

[2] G.M. was in a nursing-home at this address from 14 February to 21 April 1928. The text of this letter is taken from Hone's *Life*.

able to assist you as well as my old friend, W. K. Magee.[1]
I shall leave him £200 or so for the task, which is a light
one, and of course if you should absorb more of his time
than at first seems necessary, you will know how to
reward him.

The first job of work he will undertake will be the
publication of part of my correspondence with Dujardin.
He will translate the letters from French into English, and
he'll write a memoir.[2] He knew me in Ireland when I
came over as a sort of troubadour to help the Irish to do
the very thing they didn't want to do, which was to retain their own language. Those were days of storm and
stress that he'll be able to tell the story of from a different
point of view from the one adopted by me in *Hail and
Farewell*; and then he'll be able to say a great many things
to the right and to the left which will interest many readers.
The Brook Kerith, for instance, has never been prefaced
properly as yet. I have written for it lines of introduction,
but *The Brook Kerith*, as it is the only epical narrative in
the English language, deserves a preface of, shall we say,
ten or fifteen pages, and nobody will be able to write
these pages better than Magee. And there are a hundred
other things which I needn't worry my head about now.

Magee will be passing through London in a few days,
and I wish you would write to him at The Arlington,
Exeter Park, Central Gardens, Bournemouth, asking him
to come to see you on the subject. It would be well worth
while that you should meet and have a few words together.

Always affectionately yours George Moore

[1] Later G.M. changed his mind more than once, and his final will
(dated 30 October 1930) named Mr C. D. Medley as literary executor
and copyright-owner.

[2] This volume was published in a limited edition in 1929 (see note,
p. 173).

Thursday night [April 1928]   *7 Portland Place*

Dearest Maud,

After considering the question carefully I have come to think that the most suitable book for me to inscribe for the Prince[1] is *Avowals*. If you will send me a copy I will think out lines appropriate to the august occasion. I would write to Heinemann for a copy but fear delay. *Memoirs of my Dead Life* is out of print and I will send the Prince a copy of the new edition when it appears.

With the same affection George Moore

Sunday [Postmark 12 April 1928]   *7 Portland Place*

Dearest Maud,

I believe the operation to have been entirely successful but I am tied up like a mummy and find it hard to scribble this scribble. *Esther Waters* has been copied and Longworth will bring you a copy—he would like to, and I should like him to point out the bits that need consideration, and as you succeeded so splendidly with *The Making of an Immortal* I should cease to believe in the new thing if you did not lend your aid. The Prince wrote himself to thank me for the books I sent him. There is another thing I'd like to consult you [about] but it must keep till your return.

With all my love George Moore

[In another hand, except for last line]

20 April 1928   *7 Portland Place*

Dearest Maud,

I am sorry indeed that you are ill, and a general cold, a cold that takes you from the crown of your head to your heels, is intolerable. The cure is bed, and I hope

[1] The Prince of Wales.

163

you remain in yours. Come back as soon as you are able. London needs Freya's golden apples,[1] and none needs them so much as G.M., who seems incapable of getting out of the doctors' hands. Well indeed was "leech" the original name for doctor. They cling, oh, how they cling! How they suck! How white and bloodless they leave one! And how angry they are when we try to escape! I have contrived many escapes, but I have been caught and brought back, and on frivolous pretexts. I was going to leave to-day, but find I have to remain to learn how to wear a belt, a very complicated affair that I shall never wear. The surgeon was a storming man and strove to browbeat me, and more or less succeeded, so mighty were his threats—a real Old Testament figure. Once more—return. Only the Golden Apples can prevail. And forgive me for writing to you through a secretary. If I didn't, I should only send you a jaded, miserable letter, the offspring of a crippled pen.

With much love George Moore

[*?21 April 1928*]   *7 Portland Place*

Dearest Freya,

Come back, come back,
For we perish without thee.

George Moore

Friday 27 April [*Postmark 1928*]   *121 Ebury Street*

Dearest Maud,

Had I been able I should have written yesterday, and had I been still abler I should have taken the train at

---

[1] Freya was the Goddess of Love and Spring, who tended the garden of the gods in which grew the apples that, eaten day by day, gave eternal youth. See Wagner's *Das Rheingold*.

Victoria yesterday to meet you in Paris. But I am still an invalid and the doctors would have held up their hands saying that I was a wicked and unjust man about to let go to waste all the great and good work they had put into my body. It would have been better if I had remained another month in the Home, for to leave the Home means taking risks. I am working on *Ulick and Soracha*, fitting the story for inclusion in the *Storyteller's Holiday*,[1] and with certain emendations in my head I could bide in the Home. I love you better than ever and long to see you more than ever, which is a miracle as Summers would say.

George Moore

6 May [1928]   *121 Ebury Street*

Dearest Maud,

I am much distressed and would cross over to see you if the journey were possible, but you know it is not. I want you to outlive me by at least twenty-five years, and I want my literature to retain sufficient popularity to give you a pleasant employment—the pleasantest part of literature is not in the writing of it; and like to think of you in a room in which hang some of my pictures, arranging with Mr Longworth for new editions limited and unlimited. I like to think of you setting Longworth's advice aside and insisting that your judgment and taste shall be followed. How happy I should go to my grave if I knew these things would come to pass.

I am working now on *Ulick and Soracha*, remoulding the opening chapters (those were the faulty ones) and am confident that the story will soon be among my best things.

As ever, dearest Maud, George Moore

[1] The Uniform Edition of *A Storyteller's Holiday* (2 vols., 1928) included *Ulick and Soracha*, the dedication of which (see note, p. 140) was now transferred to the major work.

22 May [*Postmark 1928*]   *121 Ebury Street*

Dearest Maud,

I have been expecting you for the last three days. Others have come, shadows, dreams, but you are my reality. When may I see you and where—here or at Grosvenor Square?

With the longing and affection of a lifetime

George Moore

Monday [*Postmark 25 June 1928*]   *121 Ebury Street*

Dearest Maud,

I enclose a letter just received from Nancy, a very pretty letter just like herself and very like you. She is not your daughter for nothing, and having had the privilege of knowing you both I love you both. I hope to see you this week. Bridget Guinness asked me to dinner on Thursday. I hope you are of the party.

With love George Moore

Thursday [*Postmark 20 July 1928*]   *121 Ebury Street*

Dearest Maud,

I had to go to a Home on Tuesday night for a small operation. On Wednesday morning I was operated on again, with the result that I returned to Ebury Street so tired by pain that I could hardly speak. But sleep awaited me, such a sleep as I have never known before—twelve hours at least if not thirteen. If I am well enough, and I think I shall be well enough, I will come to luncheon on Saturday. Two more nights will restore me to the health and strength of everyday.

With love George Moore

166

Seaborough
Hourwood Avenue
Bournemouth

Dearest Maud,

Thank you many times for the postcard. The four-teenth-century Virgin is exquisite, and, forgetful that a century so vile had dreamed so beautifully, I return to her again and again, and to you who sent her to me. I am glad you like the *Memoirs*.[1] Between my love of art and you my life has gone by, and I often regret that I did not take more hours from art to give to you. But perhaps you saw enough of me.

With love George Moore

Write to 121 Ebury Street.

1 September 1928   *121 Ebury Street*

Dearest Maud,

I am waiting for another postcard, for the strange beauty of the Virgin's face, the commanding figure of the child and every fold of the gown falling about the knees and the bent foot awaken a pining for the refinements of feeling that animate the sculpture of the middle ages, and nowhere, to my knowledge, are these more exquisitely expressed than in the Virgin you sent me. My visit to Bournemouth brought me a renewal of health and I hope it will last long enough for me to finish *Aphrodite in Aulis*. When do you return? Do write, and believe me to be the faithfullest of lovers.   G.M.

[1] The finally revised Uniform Edition of *Memoirs of my Dead Life* was published in 1928. Lady Cunard's copy has disappeared, but her copy of the limited Moore Hall edition (1921) is inscribed: "To Lady Cunard George Moore sends this book. *Beaucoup de petits vers et une seule grande passion.* 10 October 1921."

Dearest Maud,

Le Lac Bourget[1] is as clear in my mind as your face and hands, and on reading your description of it I muttered, does she think I have forgotten Le Lac Bourget? I was irritated, but the irritation passed in the next sentence, so feelingly do you speak of the days we spent there. But I cannot trust myself to linger in the sweetness of the past, and to escape from tears will ask a favour. On your way back you will stop in Paris for a few days and I shall be glad if you will spend five pounds on a brooch suitable as a present for Clara.[2] Her heart is one of the kindest; she is an excellent cook devoted to me and I would make her a little present, a keepsake, but am no judge of jewellery. You will choose the trinket better than I. And do not delay to come to see me, for I have been too long without seeing you.

Always affectionately yours George Moore

22 September [*1928*]   *121 Ebury Street*

Dearest Maud,

That I am going to see you is truly a joyful tiding. The brooch I have in mind is one of the oval cameo brooches we used to see long ago, but do not trouble to seek a Victorian brooch, any one that you think will please Clara. I don't like very small brooches. I shall count the hours and days, they shall be the rosary of the Ebury Street hermit.   G.M.

[1] Near Aix-les-Bains, where Lady Cunard was staying.
[2] Clara Warville was G.M.'s cook-housekeeper from 1920 till his death. She contributed a brilliant chapter to Hone's *Life*.

22 October [*Postmark 1928*]   *121 Ebury Street*

Dearest Maud,

   Chagrined expresses my feelings on hearing that you
had been here whilst I was getting wet in the King's Road,
whither I had gone for a walk. On Sunday I thought for a
long time of going to see you. I like hearing you talk on
Sunday at three o'clock, but did not dare to go thither (to
your bedside) without an invitation. Clara tells me that
you propose coming to see me on Thursday. I hope you
will, but if it would suit your convenience better I'll go to
you. Clara tells me that you asked for Sir William Orpen's
address. If you meet him it will be better not to speak to
him of my wish that he should illustrate one of my books.
I am by no means sure the project will mature. I sent him
Héloïse only yesterday, so he has not come to any decision.
But should he speak to you about the matter, say all you
please to say on the subject.[1]

   With all the affection and love my human nature is
                    capable of I am yours G.M.

[*Postmark 7 November 1928*]   *121 Ebury Street*

Dearest Maud,

   I longed to call to see you on Sunday but refrained. A
case of cowardice it was. I did not dare lest my company
should weary you.
                    Always affectionately yours G.M.

Wednesday night [*Postmark 15 November 1928*]

Dearest,

   The days seem long and are wearisome when I don't
see you.   G.M.

                 [1] This project came to nothing.

                              169

Dearest Maud,

Your letter asking me to dine with you on Friday, tomorrow, arrived yesterday, and the signing of the title-page[1] for Nancy caused me to forget to send an immediate answer. I sent you a telegram however, saying it would give me much pleasure to see you again. A messenger left the sheets here but I do not know from whom he came and am in doubt if I am to bring the sheets to you to return or if I am to send them myself. If I do not hear from you to the contrary I'll forward them tomorrow, Friday, by registered post.

As always yours G.M.

The edition is printed on beautiful rag paper, the finest I have ever seen.

Dearest Maud,

When you bring a copy of *Héloïse and Abélard* for me to sign tomorrow, will you on your way hither run over in your mind the inscription you would like me to add to it. I would like the inscription to be tactful, and for this end may I say that you think a book telling of the recovery of art from the barbarism of the dark ages in the twelfth century presents some analogies to the circumstances of London in the twentieth century and may decide a waverer to join the Opera League?

I liked your dinner party on Friday night. Sir Robert

---

[1] Of a revised edition of *Peronnik the Fool*, which Nancy Cunard printed and published in a limited edition from her Hours Press in 1928. The page that G.M. signed was, in fact, the one facing the title-page. These two pages form part of a two-leaf (four-page) gathering, and the 200 copies of it are the "sheets" referred to.

Abdy endeared himself to me when he told that he bought a third folio Shakespeare in his twentieth year, paying all his available cash for it, £300. He was asked by a guest if he had sold it and answered he had not, it being his first venture. The whole man is in the anecdote. I was very sorry for coming late to dinner. You forgot to tell me your dinner was earlier than usual *or I read casually*.

Always affectionately yours George Moore.

1 January 1929   *121 Ebury Street*

Dearest Maud,

On looking through my letters I find that Mary Curzon asked me to come to see her on Thursday at 4.30, and I am sure you would not like me to disappoint her, however slight the disappointment might be; to do so would be unkind, flagrantly unkind, wherefore I propose to go with you to see the pictures early one morning next week. Eleven o'clock would be a good time: we should escape the crowd and I should have the pleasure of hearing your appreciations of the pictures. Will next Monday suit you? And would you like me to come to fetch you, or would you prefer to meet me under the portico of the Academy?[1] You were in delightful humour yesterday and our talk has ever since been murmuring on in recollections. *Aphrodite* is coming out very well, I think, and I hope to write the last chapter within the next week or two. It pleased me to hear that you liked *Peronnik*, and that you had sent it to the Prince. I am more than ever addicted to the belief that we are in for a great King, of all a great English King with a personality that is all his own, and England has had many great Kings.

Always affectionately yours George Moore

[1] Where an important exhibition of Dutch Art was on view.

11 January [Postmark 1929]   *121 Ebury Street*

Dearest Maud,

It is—it must be—a fortnight since I have seen you. But tomorrow I shall see you, hurrah!

With love G.M.

[Typewritten except for signature]

1 February 1929   *121 Ebury Street*

Dearest Maud,

The Duchess of Marlborough called here yesterday and spent some time with me talking very pleasantly, but she tells me you are not well; the flu I suppose. Shall I come and see you on Sunday? I am quite free every day now, the last chapter of *Aphrodite* has been put upon paper and a great weight taken off my mind.

Affectionately George Moore

Monday [Postmark 26 February 1929]   *121 Ebury Street*

Dearest Maud,

I returned from Kent an hour ago, where I had been spending a long week-end, and on my return I found amid a quantity of odds and ends your postcard. It gave me much pleasure to read that you thought of me sometimes, for I have been thinking of you more intensely and more constantly than usual, so it seems, and the thought of the long whiles that go by without seeing you saddens me. I am at the end of my life or nearing the end of it, and I never forget that you are the only woman that mattered. I daresay that I did not love you as well as I might have loved you, but I gave you all the love I was capable of. I never cease to think of you, and I write this to you for there are times when one feels one must tell

Lady Cunard, 1929

the truth. Yes, it is so, you are the one that I saw and heard most clearly; the others were but phantoms. We all seek and I found what I sought in you, and now I can write no more, my sadness is too deep.

Always yours George Moore

[*Postmark 19 March 1929*]

Dearest Maud,

I send you a copy of my letters to Dujardin:[1] some were written more than thirty years ago. I permitted the publication on condition that I did not see the letters. My friends often lack money and that is the true explanation. The letters are well translated I think, but the French is incorrect [in the] merely marginal verses. I think I can guess who was in my mind when I wrote the verses on p. 66.[2]

Always yours G.M.

Magee's introduction is written in very beautiful English; I don't think the English language was better written even in olden days.

[1] *Letters from George Moore to Ed. Dujardin*, 1886–1922, translated, selected, and introduced by John Eglinton (W. K. Magee), was published in a limited edition by Crosby Gaige in March 1929.

[2] These verses, sent to Dujardin on 31 July 1908, run:

> Pour voir une femme
> Qui remplit mon âme
> Vieille comme elle est
> (L'âme) de clareté—
>
> Quelle âge a la belle?
> Quelle âge a son aile?
> Son cul est-il gras?
> Cher, je ne sais pas.
> Mais la strophe est mauvaise,
> Je suis plus à l'aise
> Dans ma prose anglaise.

173

9 April 1929   *121 Ebury Street*

Dearest Maud,

Your guests arriving one after another passed me and I
inscribed the copy of *The Brook Kerith*[1] negligently. I
know now what I should have written:

> To Maud Cunard, a woman of genius. Her genius
> is manifest in her conversation, and like Jesus and
> Socrates she has refrained from the other arts.[2]

I go to Bournemouth. My house needs such a thorough
cleaning that I shall be away a fortnight.

Devotedly yours George Moore

Sunday night [? Spring 1929]   *121 Ebury Street*

Dearest Maud,

As I walked through Grosvenor Square enjoying the
blowing of the sweet south wind I remembered that
Bridget Guinness said she would call for me on Tuesday
to go to see the pictures that we saw together. Mr Morgan,
the dramatic critic of *The Times*, wrote to say that he
would bring Sheila Kaye-Smith to see me on Thursday
afternoon.[3] I have no other engagement and hope to see
you during the week.

The same as ever George Moore

[1] A new limited edition, illustrated by Stephen Gooden (1929).

[2] The inscription in Lady Cunard's copy in fact reads: "To Maud
Cunard, a woman of genius and whose genius it has been my privilege to enjoy and appreciate since I gave her *Esther Waters* many years
ago. George Moore. 7 April 1929."

[3] Mr Charles Morgan cannot remember the exact date of this
incident, but it was probably early in 1929. As this book is going to
press I learn of the existence of a copy of the Uniform Edition of
Memoirs of my Dead Life (1928) inscribed "To Sheila Kaye-Smith
whose books, especially *Green Apple Harvest*, I have read with
pleasure and admiration. George Moore. 25 July 1928." This may
indicate an earlier date for this letter, but it is possible that G.M.
sent the inscribed book before he had met the lady.

[? May 1929][1]   *121 Ebury Street*

Dearest Maud,

Now about the *Evening Standard*. You remember that
you spoke to me about the paper and asked me if I would
write something for it. If the *Evening Standard* would like
a long short story from me I will sell. *Christina Harford
and her Divorce* runs to nearly 20,000 words. There is no
scene in court, no evidence is given, merely a statement
that after the case Christina finds herself a castaway.
Christina does not become a nun but the story pursues
its way through a convent and out of it without break.
As in all my stories, everything I have to say is included in
the story. It contains no attack on anybody's religion nor
are moral questions discussed. The recommendation of
the story is its humanity. I will sell the serial rights for a
price and the price need not be a very high one. Now about
something more interesting; will you come here to
luncheon and drive with me to Dulwich? You have not
seen the gallery for many a year.

> Always affectionately yours George Moore

Sunday 26 May [*1929*]   *121 Ebury Street*

Dearest Maud,

I have so few engagements that it seems absurd to keep
an engagement book. All the same my very few engagements are hard to keep in mind whilst you are speaking,
and on Saturday it happened to me to forget one. I
remembered Monday as a plighted afternoon and forgot
that Tuesday is also plighted. But all the rest of the week
is free and Dulwich is not far from London.

> Devotedly yours George Moore

¹ The story mentioned in this letter is a complete mystery. It
certainly never appeared in the *Evening Standard*: neither G.M.'s
biographer nor his bibliographer has ever heard of it. This date is
therefore pure guesswork.

19 July [*Postmark 1929*]   *121 Ebury Street*

Dearest Maud,

This letter is commonplace in substance and intention—it is no more than one of a thousand other letters
written to tell you that I look forward to seeing you. I
have just written the scene in which Rhesos goes to the
greenwood at bidding of the oracle, hoping to see Aphrodite rise out of the waves shaking her golden locks alone
in the sunrise. Thou shalt behold her at last foam-born
Aphrodite in Aulis, he says. He is disappointed many
times, and my hope is that I shall not be disappointed
tomorrow.

Devotedly G.M.

[*July 1929*]   *121 Ebury Street*

Dearest Maud,

I have had a bit of luck and send you the news, hoping
of course to obtain your approval. I finished the writing
of the sibyl's pronouncement when Rhesos consults her
regarding his chance of recovering enough inspiration to
carve a statue of Aphrodite. I think oracularly in the
hexameters which I enclose.

With love, dearest woman, G.M.

[*Enclosed in another hand*]

Since thy quest is a pattern betake thee now to the
   green wood
Sculptor and wait her coming beneath the shadow of
   plane-trees
Shaking her golden locks exultant alone in the sunrise
Thou shalt behold her at last foam-born Aphrodite in
   Aulis.[1]

[1] See *Aphrodite in Aulis* (1930), chap. xv.

Dearest,

The Duchess telegraphed asking me for Saturday, which, if I read the telegram rightly, means a party, and a party of, shall I say, a dozen people would not be tolerable, my conditions being what they are: so I telegraphed that Saturday was engaged and wrote a longish letter explaining fully. Parties are for the young and middle-aged like other things. Do you recognise your words adapted to my case? I have not time or appetite in the afternoon for anything but my book, which must be finished before my operation.

With love to you, dear lady of my thoughts,

dear Lady Cunard, G.M.

21 October [actually September]   *121 Ebury Street*
[Postmark 1929]

Dearest Maud,

I got a card from you; it seems a long while ago, perhaps not more than a month, but ever since I have been reproaching myself for not writing. The truth is that a postcard is very little encouragement to correspondence and *Aphrodite in Aulis* has filched all my hours away, with the result however that I am now writing the last chapter. I expect to finish the book before October. The word October sets me thinking of you back in Grosvenor Square; the fine weather has passed into dark and it cannot be that you are still at St. Moritz. Need I end this letter with assurances that my affection for you is the same as it has always been.

Devotedly G.M.

Thursday   *121 Ebury Street*
[*Postmark 15 November 1929*]

My dear Maud,

You looked in your beautiful frock as enchanting as a Gavarni drawing. I'd have told you at the time but could not think what you did look like. I had to think it over.

Always affectionately yours George Moore

[*4 December 1929*][1]   *121 Ebury Street*

Dearest Maud,

Last night's assembly was typical of London Society, and I am glad I was there, for it set my thoughts flowing in a new direction. A disappointment there was—I did not get the hoped-for five minutes' talk with you. I enclose a letter from Charles Morgan, and, as you will be my literary executor, it is important that you should meet him. He mentions two dates that will suit him, and he adds that if neither suits your convenience he will be glad to fit in his arrangements with your opportunity. We can go to you or you can come here, whichever you prefer. But do fix the date, for you should meet him.

With the same affection G.M.

10 December [*1929*]

Dearest Maud,

I was pleased to get your postcard, for it assured me that you will be at the luncheon unless something unforeseen occurs—the drownding of London for instance. You will like Mr. Morgan, I think and hope; be this as it may, you will find him a useful ally.

Yours always affectionately George Moore

[1] The enclosed letter from Charles Morgan is dated Tuesday 3 December [1929].

18 February [*Postmark 1930*]　　　　*121 Ebury Street*

Dearest Maud,

The news that came today that you are too ill to see me distressed me. Pray keep me informed of your condition. Give the necessary order, for I am anxious, terribly anxious.

Devotedly G.M.

9 March [*1930*]　　　　*121 Ebury Street*

Dearest Maud,

I have finished *The Passing of the Essenes* the day before yesterday, and yesterday I felt so tired that I could not summon sufficient strength to go to see you. I could not move out of my armchair. I hadn't had a day's rest for months and the temptation was enveigling to sit by the fire and dream of you and myself.

Affectionately yours G.M.

Hoping to see you soon.

Sunday 23 [*Postmark March 1930*]　　　　*121 Ebury Street*

Dearest Maud,

I have spent the day waiting for Mr Liveright who is coming over to consider the Brentano muddle with me.[1] I have had two notes from him saying he would be with me on or about the 23rd. I hope to see you; any day that is convenient to you during the week will be convenient to me.

The same as ever G.M.

Come here if you can, for then I shall hear you talking to me.

[1] Boni & Liveright were now G.M.'s American publishers, in succession to Brentano, who had gone into liquidation.

Dearest Maud,

   Your company almost dispelled my sickness. I was
in bed at ten o'clock and after a troubled night awoke
refreshed. Your visit was a charitable act and a large part
of the day I reclined on your pillow thinking of your kindness in bringing it to me. You are all kindness, courage
and another admirable quality; "exaltation" I must write,
for the heartburn has returned and stolen the word that
was in my mind before dinner. Mr Atchley, British
Legation Athens, called at four o'clock. He wrote me
several letters about the road from Athens to Aulis and
these letters were of use to me in the composition of
Aphrodite. He begged me to tell him the story in a few
words, and this being impossible I read him the first chapter and a bit of the second to his evident pleasure. He says
the story must appear in a Greek newspaper. He has lived
in Greece for the last forty years.

The same as ever George Moore

   Liveright is coming to see me at four o'clock tomorrow.
Mr Atchley is coming at the same hour on Thursday.
"Selfhood" is nearer than exaltation.

Tuesday night [*Postmark 30 April 1930*]

Dearest Maud,

   A five minutes' visit from you is better than a thousand
luncheons. But if you think I am needed in Saturday's
social scheme I'll come—in other words I'll come if I do
not hear to the contrary.

With the same affection George Moore

Barton is seeking an ideal cast.[1] But no words about this on Saturday.

12 May [Postmark 1930]   *121 Ebury Street*

Dearest Maud,

I go to 29 Wimpole Street to meet Sir John Thomson Walker tomorrow who will give me an odious potion that will put my kidney to the test. I shall be at 29 Wimpole Street for two nights—I can tell you no more, but needless to say that I shall be glad to see you on Thursday. I have just received a telegram from Barton: "Trying arrange production June. If impossible must postpone till Autumn." I am writing to Gustav Holst about the music. Dear Maud, I love you more than I ever did, and I always loved you.

The same as ever only more so George Moore

24 June [Postmark 1930]   *121 Ebury Street*

Dearest Maud,

I can do only one thing at a time, and when you are here there is but you to hear and to see, and this being so the marvellous orchid bloomed unobserved or almost, but you had not gone many minutes before I sat absorbed. A marvellous bloom—an unearthly bloom of mauve, and the aspiring fern increases the wonder; a sort of miniature fir-tree it is.

Dearest woman, how can I thank? You cannot tell me and I cannot imagine, for I have no more love to give; you had it all years and years ago, but with the same love I am

Yours always George Moore

[1] Lionel Barton was the manager of the Arts Theatre, where G.M.'s play *The Passing of the Essenes* was to be produced, with incidental music by Gustav Holst, on 1 October 1930.

I walked twice round Belgrave Square last evening with the best results. I recommend the square to you when insomnia becomes unbearable. I will accompany you.

Thursday evening   *121 Ebury Street*
[*Postmark 27 June 1930*]

Dearest Maud,

I am sorry I did not acquit myself satisfactorily at your luncheon, but the fact is I am not feeling very well, I need change of air and long absence from the writing table. Tomorrow I have an appointment with Sir John Thomson Walker in the afternoon, and on Saturday I have to see Albery, the owner of the Arts Theatre, but on Sunday I am free, altogether free, and sight of you would help to restore my confidence in the pleasure of living. Today I was not myself, but on Sunday I shall be glad to go for a drive with you or spend half an hour over the teacups with you. My visit to Paris will not be a long one; I shall often think of you and Nancy. There is much to be said in praise of her two poems. Her words are her own and they are rich, varied and well chosen.

I shall write her an encouraging letter; an encouraging letter means a great deal to the striver and this time Nancy has striven.

Always yours, dear Maud. I am not to blame for today's depression of spirit.

George Moore

[*on back of envelope*]

Your bloom flourishes, a joy for ever apparently.

G.M.

28 June [Postmark 1930]   *121 Ebury Street*

Dearest Maud,

Your orchid seems to be endowed with a longevity that I cannot help comparing to—I leave you to finish the phrase. Hoping to see you tomorrow I am

always affectionately yours G.M.

Wednesday 2 July [Postmark 1930]   *Hotel Continental*
Paris

Dearest Maud,

I got a telephone message yesterday saying I was to speak with you between two o'clock and half past. The heat is great; I fell asleep while waiting, and on waking at three o'clock in despair I made many enquiries but met with the same answer everywhere: "There has been no call." Somebody has blundered, but whether the blunderer is I or the telephonist I cannot say. I regret I missed the pleasure of your voice, and the news, should your news be good news; my hope is that serious consequences are not involved in the mistake.

Always affectionately yours George Moore

Sunday   *The Crest House*
[Postmark 17 August 1930]   *Weybridge*

Dearest Maud,

I am here since yesterday with Sir Horace Plunkett,[1] and am returning to London to continue *A Lost Masterpiece*.[2] I called at No 7 Grosvenor Square and got some news of you from your blond and always gracious butler,

[1] Irish statesman and agricultural reformer (1854–1932).

[2] On 4 August 1930 G.M. referred to the opening pages of this never-finished story in a letter to A. J. A. Symons.

and from him I learnt that you were moving about from town to town and would not return till the middle of October, and from Sir Horace I learnt the surprising news that he had not had the pleasure of meeting you; he proposed that you and I should come to his delightful hilltop in October. Nancy left London without coming to bid me goodbye, which was unkind. I received a setting of the hymn the Essenes sing as they cross the stage, about twenty bars. I have no other news. I love you as much as ever, but that is not news to you.

With the same affection George Moore

[*Typewritten except for first and last lines*]

30 August 1930   *121 Ebury Street*

Dearest Maud,

I am obliged to write to you through a secretary, for I have not the strength to-day to write a long letter with my own hand. I went to Weybridge for a week-end and came back with a most frightful cold which doesn't leave me. I suppose it will leave me, but at present it is stuck fast. The heat is overpowering, and how the day will go by God knows. 93 in the shade in Ebury Street is no joke. Well, to come to what I have to say. I shall be much obliged if you will send me a guide book that gives an account of Arles. I am not interested in the great Roman amphitheatre but in the fact that Mistral, the great Provençal poet, lived there and wrote in a shieling by the wayside his immortal poem entitled *Mireille*. Every guide book containing an account of Arles cannot fail to tell me some facts about Mistral, when he was born, when he died, whether he ever wrote any other works but *Mireille*, and so forth. I should like, too, to see a portrait of him—any sort of photograph; these must be easily procurable.

I needn't say that my time hangs heavily since you left

London. The production of *The Passing of the Essenes* is advertised for the first of October. You will be back by then, I hope. To-morrow, if the heat disperses, I will write you a pleasanter letter than this one.

With much love George Moore

8 August [actually September] [1930]   *121 Ebury Street*

Dearest Maud,

Many thanks for the life of Mistral. But do you not waste any time trying to read *Mireille*. It differs very little from the Christmas cards already published and from those waiting to be published. After reading three cantos I felt like a man who was invited out to luncheon and instead of being offered a wing of chicken or a cutlet was handed a baby's bottle and asked to take a pull.

With the same affection G.M.

Thursday   *Le Coin-sur-Juine*
[Postmark 9 October 1930]   *Lardy*
Seine-et-Oise

Dearest Maud,

I am sorry to hear of your illness and I figure you lying lonely in a great German hotel—you do too much; quiet is what you need. From the length of your letter I gather that you are on your way back to health and will be in London at the end of the month. If you are there on the 29th you will arrive in time for the revival of *The Passing of the Essenes*—a letter having just come from Bronson Albery asking my permission to revive the play. I shall attend. I have not yet seen the play, only a few rehearsals. But the production is said to be very fine. The Arts is certainly stepping out.

Always affectionately yours George Moore

24 October 1930   *121 Ebury Street*

Dearest Maud,

I did not close my eyes last night, and am too tired to write a letter. I should much like to know when you are returning to London. My play is being revived next Tuesday for seven performances. Will you be present then, or would a later date suit you better? Send me a card, please.

The same as ever George Moore

28 October [Postmark 1930]   *121 Ebury Street*

Dearest Maud,

There is no mystery, but a very commonplace story that needs for comprehensibility at least four pages of letter paper, large size, written small and closely. You would have looked upon me as the greatest bore in Christendom. I look forward to seeing you tomorrow, Wednesday.

With the same affection George Moore

Tuesday night [? 4 November 1930]   *121 Ebury Street*

Dearest Maud,

Sometimes I am moody, even a trifle sulky, but you bring sunshine wherever you go, and I listen in dread lest the secretary should return and break the enchanted spell. I would remain with you though my head be brimming with story. Come again and in your car to take me for a drive . . . Alas my afternoons are spent with secretary. Her mornings belong to Mrs Belloc Lowndes. What is to be done?

I enclose the article *The Times Literary Supplement* published. Please to return it when read. I have to send it to France.[1]

With the same affection G.M.

8 December [Postmark 1930]　　　　　　　*121 Ebury Street*

Dearest Maud,

I have not seen you for a month, which is such a long while that I frequently ask myself if the end of our friendship has come at last.

Nancy came here to lunch on Saturday.

Always devotedly yours George Moore

[Typewritten except for first and last lines]

27 December 1930　　　　　　　*121 Ebury Street*

Dearest Maud,

I should have written to you before if I had not been incapacitated from writing by illness. I have been in the hands of a nurse for the last three nights, but am better now. My complaint was a chill on the bladder.

You were kind enough to send me a box of cigars, but they are black and strong and bitter as rock salt. I smoked half a cigar and wrapped the remaining half in paper and returned it to the box, and I am writing to ask you from whom you bought the cigars, for there is little doubt that the tobacconist will be glad to exchange this box for another containing fine, blond, mild cigars.

If you have time, come and see your poor old wreck.

With the same affection George Moore

[1] On 30 October 1930 *The Times Literary Supplement* printed a letter by G.M. on *The Passing of the Essenes*, which was used as the Preface to the Uniform Edition of the play (1931).

[Postcard. Postmark 1 January 1931]

It will be a treat indeed to see you if the interview endures but a few minutes. I have not seen anybody for a fortnight and have been sick all the time.

Always affectionately yours G.M.

Tuesday evening [? *April 1931*]   *121 Ebury Street*

Dearest Maud,

I hope Heinemann sent you a copy of *The Untilled Field*. I ordered it to be sent to you, and I enclose the last letter I received about the little song that has pleased many.[1] I paid a visit to St James's Palace this morning, and the Prince talked with me for nearly an hour, and when we meet I'll try to tell you about the visit.

Devotedly yours G.M.

9 May 1931   *121 Ebury Street*

Dearest Maud,

For the last twenty-five years I have looked to you as the one capable and trustworthy person, who could and would direct the publication of my writings after my death, Heinemann advising you on technical points just as he advises me. I have never met with opposition from Mr Evans, i.e. Heinemann, and you will not meet with any. That you should have to consult anybody else would be intolerable. It has always been in my mind too that the task would be agreeable to you. Besides the narratives, conversations and essays there is a play, *The Passing of the Essenes*. I have just finished a revision of the text for

[1] Heinemann published a new, revised, edition of *The Untilled Field* in April 1931. The music of the shepherd's song appears on pp. 276-77.

publication this season and was much impressed by the beauty of the design and the text. This play will be remembered; all that is unique persists, and it is about this play that I wish to speak with you. There is the comedy, *The Making of an Immortal*, a trifle that need not occupy us.

With the same affection George Moore

Sunday 10 May [Postmark 1931]   *121 Ebury Street*

Dearest Maud,

I wrote to you on Saturday but I fear my letter was posted too late to reach you on Saturday night; you will receive it tomorrow morning, Monday. You will notice that I agree with you that the bequest would be useless if you were not given a free hand to arrange for all subsequent editions of my writings, Evans advising you as he advises me; my powers will be transferred to you, that is all. But there is another matter about which I wish to consult you, the play entitled *The Passing of the Essenes*. This play contains some of my best writing and of a certainty it will be produced again. We are moving into times when a play cannot be banned. And it is about the performance of this play that I wish to speak to you. I am engaged tomorrow at 4.30 but any other day of the week and at the hour that conveniences you best, here or at 7 Grosvenor Square. I am in much better health and am pleased with what I am writing and it will be no trouble for me to go to you. But do write making an appointment.

With the same affection George Moore

[Postmark 14 May 1931]   *121 Ebury Street*

Dearest Maud,

Your stubborn silence leaves little doubt that you do not wish to associate yourself with my literature; I thought of you as a literary trustee of genius, but it would seem that your mind has changed and far be it from me to try to persuade you against your better reason . . .

A message has just come from you inviting me to lunch on Saturday. I accept, but not with the view of trying to persuade you. Perhaps the need of the occasion might be met by your coming here to choose and to take away a picture from my walls. But always, dear friend, according to your desire.

With the same affection George Moore

3 June [Postmark 1931]   *121 Ebury Street*

My Dearest Maud,

It was kind of you to come to fetch me for a drive today but you are always kind and good, and when I am with you the thought entertains me all the while, that I am the luckiest man in the world. My address in Bournemouth will be for the next three weeks: Miss Gaddie, 29 Grand Avenue, Bournemouth.

The same as always George Moore

Sunday [Postmark 6 July 1931]   *121 Ebury Street*

Dearest Maud,

Yesterday I was out of my humour and did not think it safe to remain within doors. The air refreshed me and I returned home disappointed I had missed you, and full of recollections of the afternoon we had spent in Richmond Park I mused the time away. I thought of calling on you between three and four o'clock; at that time your guests are leaving; but Ovaltine does not always procure sleep and I felt I must doze.

With the same affection George Moore

Wednesday night   *121 Ebury Street*
[*Postmark 16 July 1931*]

Dearest Maud,

I hope to see you before you leave London. If I don't I
shall be disappointed, very disappointed. Tomorrow
afternoon I have some friends coming to see me—friends
of yours, Lady Desborough and Maurice Baring. Come
if it pleases you to come. I'll be glad but will not pretend
that a drive with you in Richmond Park or elsewhere
with you on Sunday would [not] be preferable.

The same as ever George Moore

23 August [*Postmark 1931*]   *121 Ebury Street*

Dearest Maud,

I have not got time to write a gossipy letter and I am
glad, for my pen might betray me; even if it were written
harmless I should begin to suspect it when it was in the
post. I send you the *Times* review of *Aphrodite*. The book
did not move you but it seems to have found many ad-
mirers.[1]

The same as ever George Moore

[*Typewritten except for signature*]

29 October 1931   *121 Ebury Street*

Dearest Maud,

Many thanks for the book. Gooden wrote this morning
to say he was very pleased with it, and was going to submit a list of passages for illustration to Harrap.[2]

[1] The Uniform Edition (1931). *Aphrodite in Aulis* was originally
published in a limited edition in December 1930. It was dedicated to
Sir John Thomson-Walker.

[2] A new edition of *Peronnik the Fool*, with engravings by Stephen
Gooden, was published by Harrap in 1933, after G.M.'s death, though
the copies were signed by him and by Gooden. The closing lines of *A
Communication To My Friends* (1933) are in praise of these engravings.

Do not forget Saturday. I shall expect you as soon as you can escape from your luncheoners, about three o'clock.

Always affectionately yours George Moore

[*Typewritten except for signature*]

9 November 1931   *121 Ebury Street*

Dearest Maud,

You remember that my quarrel with Nancy was about some lines that I gave her and which she afterwards wanted me to sign; but I had to refuse to sign them, for I could not resign myself to making money out of such a trivial scrap of literature—about ten or twelve lines entitled, perhaps, *A Dream in a Forest*, or *The Poet and the Pine*.

If you have a copy of this, shall I say prose-poem, will you send it to me, for I am in need of it at the present moment.[1]

The same as ever George Moore

[*Typewritten except for first and last lines*]

15 January 1932   *121 Ebury Street*

Dearest Maud,

Your letter was very welcome; I was beginning to think I had lost you—a familiar dread. But since I have not, let me know when you are in England, for I am longing to see you.

[1] This fragment, *The Talking Pine*, was printed, but never published, by Nancy Cunard at the Hours Press. It appears in her book, *G.M.: Memories of George Moore* (1956), where an account of the "quarrel" can also be found. G.M. probably wanted a copy for Lady Cynthia Asquith, who included it in her anthology *The Silver Ship* (1932).

If I am writing to you through a secretary it is because I am persecuted with insomnia, complicated by sciatica. I should go for a walk, the air would do me good, but I have not got the will to go to the street or to the writing table.

With the same affection George Moore

[*Typewritten except for first and last lines*]

8 March 1932   *121 Ebury Street*

Dearest Maud,

I was sorry not to be able to assist at your luncheon party last Saturday; my infirmity does not permit me, for the moment at least, to go about and see my friends: I am a prisoner in my armchair, quite well, but a prisoner.

If you can manage, as you whirl through Belgravia, to stop at my door it would help me to endure the passing hours of the days.

With the same affection George Moore

Sunday night [*? April 1932*]   *121 Ebury Street*

Dearest Maud,

It is like you to send your car to fetch me, but I could not summon enough courage to face a drawing room full of people. I need Dr Oreste's name and address; he will be able to direct me to somebody in Paris who can insert a tube unfailingly. Sir John Thomson Walker could but he practises no longer. There must be another who can adjust a tube but I do not know his name nor his number.

With the same affection G.M.

16 April [? *1932*]

My dear Maud,

I am sorry, but I do not feel well enough this afternoon. If you will send me Dr Oreste's address I shall be glad and thank you many times for your kindness.

Affectionately yours G.M.

[*Postmark 24 June 1932*]   *121 Ebury Street*

Dearest Maud,

I am afraid I cannot come to luncheon tomorrow, Saturday, and am very unhappy about it. Perhaps your unfailing good nature will bring you here one day next week. The briefest visit will cheer me, the sight of your face will be a help.

With the same affection George Moore

14 October 1932   *121 Ebury Street*

Dearest Maud,

If you will read Chapters xxi and xxii of *Héloïse and Abélard* attentively I think you will agree that nobody has written better, but these pages must be read line by line; a book has no more to give than the reader brings to it. The pages that captured my admiration are those that tell of Jean Guiscard's entry into the tavern, his hat on the back of his head, talking loudly of the questions that would be debated at Franchard. In the woods round Franchard you will meet the hermit, who is I masquerading under the name of Gaucelm d'Arembert, and yourself under the name of the Lady Malberge.[1] I look forward to lunching

---

[1] The relevant passages from chap. xxii of *Héloïse and Abélard* (Uniform Edition, 1925) are given on pp. 196-200. Allowing for G.M.'s habit of weaving fact into fiction, they probably present the closest account he ever published of his love for Lady Cunard.

with you on Saturday. I have many agreeable and wise things to say to you and hope you will allow me to say some of them.

> With the same affection George Moore

[*Typewritten except for signature*]

2 January 1933   *121 Ebury Street*

Dearest Maud,

I hope your cold is better and that you will soon be able to come to see me. I see nobody except an occasional interviewer and then I have to tell him a number of facts about the book I am writing—*A Communication to my Friends.*[1]

> With the same affection George Moore

[1] Begun as a General Introduction to the Uniform Edition of his works, this essay grew under G.M.'s hand into a projected book on its own. He worked on it to within a few days of his death, and the resulting fragment was published in a limited edition by the Nonesuch Press on 13 June 1933. Later in the same year it was put to its original use in the volume of the Uniform Edition which contained *A Mummer's Wife.*

Abélard . . . asked the hermit what great spiritual crisis
compelled him to live apart from the Lady Malberge,
whom he understood to be none other than the Vicom-
tesse de Chatelleraud. But I do not live apart; she is
always with me, and that she should never be far from
me is my reason for having withdrawn myself from
her. . . . I am Gaucelm d'Arembert, whose soul is well
known to be the Lady Malberge. I cannot call my love
of her anything else, for it abides when all other things
have passed, and day by day it grows clearer to me and
nearer to me, and the soul, we have always been told, is
what is most essential in us. If that be so, and who will
say it is not, Malberge is my soul, for nothing is essential
in me except her. Without her I should not have been
myself, and were she taken from me I should be nothing;
therefore I say, and not without reason, it seems to me,
that the Lady Malberge is my soul. Or my love of her is
my soul, if your mood, sir, is to split hairs. But, said
Abélard, the soul is all spirit. My love is all spirit, Gaucelm answered. Was your love then unfleshly? Abélard
asked. By no means; it was in my lady's bed that I came
to know myself. I was nothing before I entered it,
merely a man given over to vain commerce with every
woman that took his fancy. And you have never wavered
from your love? Abélard inquired. Wavered from my love?
You might as well ask if I have wavered from my senses.
All I see and hear is my Lady Malberge. She is the bird
that sings within me; she is the fruit that I taste—— In
memory, Abélard interposed. Memory is the truer

reality, Gaucelm answered. She is the flower that I meet upon my way and that I gather, and for each flower I gather another springs up in its place, the same flower sometimes or else a more beautiful flower than the one I have gathered. . . . But, said Abélard, . . . we would wish to hear you on this subject to which you have dedicated your life. To which, Gaucelm answered, I would devote many lives, had I many for giving, for all that is not Malberge is death. Many of us live without suspicion of the real life. It was so with me; for twenty years I was without it, living on rinds and shucks and husks, but when I met Malberge I began to live the essential life. For ten years I have lived with her in what is known as reality, and ever since have been living it in a memory which is even sweeter than the reality. But how, good hermit, did this good fortune come about? Abélard asked. There were twenty years—— That I was without knowledge of Malberge, the hermit interrupted. Yes, if we begin to count our life from the eighteenth year, for I was thirty-eight before my eyes were won by her beauty and my ears ravished by her voice, for Malberge's voice is—— Good hermit, tell us, Abélard intervened, of how you met the Lady Malberge. At a tournament it was, good sirs, in which another knight was to carry her colours; but after a few words with me her fancy changed, and she said that I should wear her colours; and when it was pointed out to her by her first husband (Malberge has been wedded twice), that she could not put aside the knight she had chosen, she answered him, saying: The tournament is given in my honour, therefore my mind may change as it pleases, and I will not sit on the balcony and watch the knights charging each other in the lists if Gaucelm d'Arembert does not wear my colours; here is my sleeve for him. And she cut her sleeve from her gown and gave it to me, and all were

197

amazed. But she would have her way, and her sleeve pinned upon my arm gave it such great favour that I overthrew all. That day none could withstand my prowess. And next day when I went to the Lady Malberge to return to her her sleeve, she raised her face to mine, and when our lips met in a kiss all my nature took fire, and the flame that was lighted that day shall never be quenched.

The fire still smoulders under the ashes of many years; stir it and it will flame again. Your questions bring it all back to me, and that is why I have not sent you away and retired into meditation of the great benefits I have received from my dear lady. But how, good hermit, did it fall out, Abélard asked, that on the death of her first husband, or divorce, whichever happened that separated them one from another, you did not wed the Lady Malberge? Our wedding was often in our minds, but I felt, and Malberge shared my belief, that love could not exist in marriage, and I said to her: Malberge, if I wed thee thou wilt hate me in six months, but if we are wise and stint our desires to blessed adultery, our love shall last to the end of our lives. . . . For two years during the life of her first husband I lived in the memory of my last meeting with Malberge, and each time I entered the Lady Malberge's bed it seemed to me more clear than the last time that it was not a mortal woman I lay down beside, but divinity, Venus herself, and our union was, or seemed to me to be, which is the same thing, a sacramental deed, in harmony with the universe and part of it. You will think me mad, good sirs, but that is a matter for your concern rather than mine, whose only care now is to discover the truth about myself and the Lady Malberge— my foible, and the last one. A pleasure it is to speak of her to you, for I am without any company except the birds and the beasts of these woods, and the castle servants, who bring me presents of food from Malberge, and the peasants from whom I buy it, therefore I thank you for having allowed me the privilege of speaking the truth to you. Does Malberge come to visit you here in your hermitage? Does she sit and talk with you of the days when you loved each other? Abélard asked. Malberge, the hermit answered, speaks very little of the days when we loved each other, and methinks she cares little to hear me remind her of them; but she comes to see me and I possess her affection, and there is little that I might ask that she would not do for me. And never during all those years did another woman tempt you? Rodebœuf inquired, feeling that he had been for a long time like one forgotten. My good sir, he who has enjoyed divinity turns aside from merely mortal woman. And was Malberge as faithful to you, sir, as you were to her? Rodebœuf asked. Eighteen years lay between me and Malberge. She was twenty when I was thirty-eight, and her imagination was as mine was in my youth. Men captured her imagination as women captured mine. Thou wilt not chide me if I spend part of to-morrow with a certain knight? she said to me. And I answered: Malberge, I hear thee with a certain sorrow, but thou canst not be else than what thou art, and if thou wert else I might not love thee. So be thyself. My prudence was rewarded, for after a very little while she quitted the new knight. It has fallen out that Malberge has wept naked in my arms, telling me that I must help her to obtain some man who had caught her fancy, reminding me of our long love, her tears flowing on her cheeks. Thou wilt help me, she has said, for I must have both of you. One is not enough, I must have both, I must live with both of you; and on these words she surrendered her beautiful body to me and her tears were forgotten . . . sometimes I mingle with the crowd and catch sight of her, and sometimes a whim brings her here to me, and I look upon my life as it has come to me through Malberge as a perfect gift. My death, which cannot be far away now, only affects me in this much, that I shall not see Malberge any more; and not seeing her, I shall be indifferent to all things after death as I am during life, indifferent to all things but Malberge.

And on these words Gaucelm d'Arembert turned away, thinking that he had said enough.

EPILOGUE

GEORGE MOORE died at 121 Ebury Street on 21 January 1933, aged eighty. He bequeathed the portrait of his grandfather by Thomas Wyatt (the only object that survived the destruction of Moore Hall) to the National Gallery of Ireland in Dublin, and a small Constable landscape to his friend and executor Mr C. D. Medley. All his other pictures, together with his furniture, books, and other belongings, he left to Lady Cunard.

She died at the Dorchester Hotel on 10 July 1948, aged seventy-five. All her fortune and belongings, including what she had inherited from George Moore, she left in equal parts to her daughter Nancy, to Lady Diana Cooper, and to Sir Robert Abdy, except for her remaining letters from George Moore which she bequeathed to Mr Sacheverell Sitwell. On July 12 *The Times* wrote of her:

. . . Small and fair and invariably dressed in the latest fashion (she once told an interviewer that her dressmaker's bill might run into thousands and that, as she was generally in a hurry, she would order ten or twenty dresses at once, wear perhaps two, and give the rest away!), Lady Cunard was probably the most lavish hostess of her day, and through her patronage of the best musical talent at her house might be met, and often heard, practically every musical celebrity, especially at her musical suppers, which were famous. She contributed £1,000 to the Imperial League of Opera in 1928 and had much to do with the launching of that ambitious enterprise, which, in spite of her enthusiastic support, met the fate common to most musical ventures at that time. Undeterred by this, she joined with Mr F. A. Szarvasy and Sir Thomas Beecham in founding the New Opera Syndicate in 1933. At her house in

Grosvenor Square the first performance of André Obey's opera, *Venus and Adonis*, was heard, and she was a liberal patron of the French "Compagnie des Quinze" that delighted intelligent playgoers in London in the early nineteen-thirties. At the opera she always occupied what was known as the omnibus box, usually surrounded by a host of friends.

Outstanding though her services to the arts were, she could not have achieved half that she did without a social gift which combined gracious sympathy with a salty yet never malicious wit. She had friends in all walks of life and was able with little apparent effort to put them at ease with themselves and with one another. One of the charms of the great parties she delighted to give was that one never knew who one would meet at them. Statesmen, poets, novelists, financiers gladly accepted her invitations and never felt their time in her company to be other than the great pleasure it was. George Moore was a constant companion of hers for many years and her influence and charm have been recorded in their autobiographical works by Sir Osbert Sitwell and Mr Harold Acton among others.[1] Her like will hardly be seen again in the years ahead and she did much to deserve her place in the social and artistic history of her time.

On July 17 the same paper published this tribute from Mr Sacheverell Sitwell:

Your generous and kind tribute to Lady Cunard only needs a few more notes of detail. Her elegant and sprightly person, of gossamer texture, concealed a mind occupied night after night with serious reading during the long hours while she was sleepless. Shakespeare and Balzac she knew in their entirety; she had read many Greek and Latin writers, in translation, and a greater part of the French and English literature of three centuries. To those who loved her it was a constant delight to watch her wits at play. Often she would hold a dinner-party audience entranced for an hour or more with her high spirits, which were of differing depths and speeds; solid, as when she spoke in the vein of the hostesses in *Lady Windermere's Fan* or *The Importance of Being Earnest*—had she

[1] See *Great Morning* by Osbert Sitwell (1948), pp. 251–53, and *Memoirs of an Aesthete* by Harold Acton (1948), pp. 212–22.

not been to Mallarmé's evenings, been drawn by Whistler, known Wilde and Beardsley?—or through the varying degrees of Lilliputian mock-heroic, fashionable persiflage, or airy nothingness of which she was the master. It must be conceded, too, that on occasion she could be a little indiscreet, though, even so, the sensation was as though you were overhearing the conversation at a game of cards in some rarefied world of elegance. Her art of conversation, nevertheless, was that of a new continent and of an American, but of an American who like herself had a grandmother who was French.

Perhaps she was at her happiest, conversationally, with an audience of an ambassador or two, a statesman, and a few young persons chosen for their inconsequence. The old would feel young and careless, and the young would feel they were being consulted upon affairs of State. When she came back from New York to London in 1942 she was not in the least daunted by the bombs, and her bravery never left her in her last illness. She will be missed, and never forgotten, by her friends of three generations. The writer of these lines was taken to her box at Covent Garden when he was a schoolboy during the last great pre-war season of 1914, and he went with her to the revival of *Boris Godunov* less than two months ago. It is dreadful to think one will never feel her light touch again, or experience her deeds of kindness. She loved to give presents, but hated to be given them. Her love for music I have scarcely mentioned, for it is so well known. I think that the sort of world in which she would like to wake from death, and find herself, is that of *The Tale of Genji*, which has been so beautifully translated into English by Mr Arthur Waley. Those who loved her will miss her wit and subtlety and nuance, will mourn her company, and think of her at concerts, in theatres, above all at the opera. This was what she loved most, and perhaps it took the place, for her, of religion.

INDEX

207